"Reading Sr. Melannie's insightful, practical, and personally challenging book made me, as one of her professors at the Institute of Formative Spirituality, feel profoundly happy. She not only learned but clearly lives Father Adrian van Kaam's insistence that each human being must pursue over a lifetime his or her unique, communal life call. Sister's commitment to the spirituality of everydayness is ample testimony to her study in this field and to her ability to reformulate creatively its seminal concepts. I recommend this book to beginners on the path as well as to people more advanced in the spiritual life."

Susan Muto, Ph.D.
Co-Founder and Executive Director
Epiphany Association
Pittsburgh, PA

"Health is not a cultural trait today, and unhealthy spirituality only adds to the confusion, especially when it offers itself as wisdom. This fine book is a very healthy and wise response to our need. Melannie Svoboda gives some excellent criteria to help us separate the wheat from the chaff."

Richard Rohr, O.F.M.
Albuquerque, NM

"Sr. Melannie Svoboda's *Traits of a Healthy Spirituality* is a solid and reliable contribution to the spirituality field. It is down-to-earth, readable and helpful to those of us who take our spiritual life seriously. Sr. Melannie calls on her wide reading and her experience as a spiritual director and novice director to describe some twenty traits of a healthy spirituality.

"Each chapter begins with pithy quotes relating to one of the traits, e.g., self-esteem, wonder, friendship, prayer, joy, freedom, etc. and then discusses the trait in a way that speaks to the reader. At the end of each chapter she poses some questions for personal reflection. I can recommend this book to anyone searching for a healthy spirituality."

William A. Barry, S.J.
The Society of Jesus
Boston, MA

"Sr. Melannie's serious and thoughtful book is a timely reminder that spirituality can easily become eccentric and unhealthy. Her experience and wisdom are evident throughout as she offers sound advice about how to avoid such a tragedy. At the same time, she delights the reader with a playful humor as she demonstrates that being serious doesn't necessarily mean being solemn."

Demetrius Dumm, O.S.B.
Author, *Flowers in the Desert* and *Cherish Christ Above All*

"This is a very healthy book. It presents an intriguing list of 20 elements in a healthy well-rounded spirituality. While integrating the wisdom of humanistic psychology with sound Christian spirituality, Sr. Svoboda focuses clearly on the initiative of God's intimately personal love. She provides a wonderful form of consciousness exam regarding God's intimate desire for a glorious fullness that constantly entices all our hearts."

George Aschenbrenner, S.J.
Jesuit Center for Spiritual Growth

"Melannie Svoboda's *Traits of a Healthy Spirituality* puts forth ways of evaluating whether or not we are progressing in that fundamental 'right relationship' between our inner and outer realities. While being both comforting and challenging, hers is a spirituality that is built on connectedness rather than law conformity or a mere desire for justice. It seemed to me that her 'traits of spirituality' were all attempts at becoming aware of and sustaining healthfully our connectedness with the Divine, with ourselves, and with each other. This is a meditative book that I would not hesitate to recommend to anyone who takes spirituality seriously."

Richard J. Gilmartin, Ph.D.
Author, *Pursuing Wellness, Finding Spirituality*

"With clarity, depth, and conviction, Sr. Svoboda calls the reader to self-reflection essential to spiritual growth. Her provocative blend of quotes and stories from traditional and contemporary spiritual masters, scripture, and wisdom culled from personal experience challenges a stagnant faith vision. Anyone interested in spirituality will find *Traits of A Healthy Spirituality* a rich source of guidance, encouragement, and joyful inspiration."

Wayne Simsic
Author, *Songs of Sunrise, Seeds of Prayer*

TRAITS
of a
HEALTHY
SPIRITUALITY

Melannie Svoboda, SND

TWENTY-THIRD PUBLICATIONS
Mystic, CT 06355

Second printing 1997

Twenty-Third Publications
185 Willow Street
P.O. Box 180
Mystic, CT 06355
(860) 536-2611
800-321-0411

ISBN 0-89622-698-0
Library of Congress Catalog Card Number 96-60346
Printed in the U.S.A.

Dedication

To Mary Ann Svoboda Hartman
my sister and best friend
(so much like me, it's uncanny,
so different, it's fun!)

Contents

Traits of a Healthy Spirituality

Introduction

When I was teaching high school, a student would sometimes come to me after school and ask, "How am I doing in your class, Sister?" I could answer that question easily, even without reaching for my grade book. I would simply ask the student several questions: What grades did you receive on your last few tests and quizzes? Were your homework assignments completed and handed in on time? Do you participate regularly in our class discussions?

The student's answers to these questions (provided the student's memory was good and perception was accurate) were good indicators of just how well (or how poorly) the student was doing in my class.

As we travel along on our journey of faith, we sometimes find ourselves asking the same question, "How am I doing?" Or, more specifically, we find ourselves wondering, "How healthy is my spirituality? How authentic is my Christian faith?"

Some people might object to such questioning. They would say that, when it comes to living our faith, we should not concern ourselves with how well we are doing. For such a concern already betrays an unhealthy spirituality—one that focuses too much on our own efforts to do good and too little on God's gratuitous love for us. Although there may be some truth to that, I still maintain it is important for us to ask, "How healthy is my spirituality?" and to ask it on a regular basis.

Why? For two main reasons. First because the history of Christianity is filled with examples of individuals and groups who, in the very name of spirituality, did some pretty foolish or even downright terrible things. Some so-called spiritual people

1

beat their bodies with scourges or engaged in debilitating fasting in the name of spirituality. Others refused to bathe for years allegedly to prove their love for God. Still others marched into foreign lands, wielding swords and waging war against people they labeled "heathens," slaughtering thousands of innocent people—all in the name of Christ. Even in our own day we find some so-called Christian groups preaching hatred and advocating violence. History is clear: the spirituality of Christians has not always been healthy. On the contrary, sometimes it has been sick. Very sick. All of which reminds us that just because we think we are following Jesus does not mean we actually are.

There is a second reason why we should periodically appraise the health of our spirituality: Jesus wants and needs us to be spiritually healthy. Before his ascension into heaven, Jesus gave his disciples (and us!) this command: "Go therefore and make disciples of all nations" (Mt 28:19). Christianity, by its very nature, is an evangelizing religion, one that calls us to witness to and share with others the good news we ourselves have heard and on which we stake our lives. The more authentic our faith, the better will be our discipleship. The healthier our spirituality, the more effective will be our witness to Jesus in our home, workplace, parish, local community, and world.

It makes sense, then, that we regularly assess the health of our spirituality. Doing so, of course, is not as easy as judging how well we may be faring in a particular class. Nevertheless, there are some fairly good indicators—some traits, if you will—of a healthy spirituality.

This book focuses on twenty such traits. I am not implying that these are the only traits of a healthy spirituality. In fact, I encourage readers to generate other traits as they read this book. Furthermore, I am not saying that we have to have all of these traits in order to have a healthy Christian spirituality. None of us is perfect. What I am suggesting, however, is this: in order to have a healthy Christian spirituality, we must give evidence of at least some of these traits. Those traits that are underdeveloped or lacking in our lives might signal the areas in which we are being called to grow.

In this regard it is good for us to recall that even the greatest saints did not evince all of these traits to the same degree in their lives. Some saints, for example, were known for their endurance of adversity while others are remembered for their show of playfulness. Some saints incarnated the virtues of meekness and patience while others exemplified zeal and passion. Christian spirituality is not monolithic. Rather, it allows for a delightful variety of nuance, texture, and shading.

The chapters in this book consist of meditations on the traits of a healthy spirituality, followed by questions for personal reflection and a suggested practice. Each chapter incorporates scripture and concludes with a prayer that focuses on its respective trait. The book can be used for personal prayer and reflection as well as for group sharing.

"How am I doing?" we ask. In one way, a better question might be, "What is God doing in my life?" For ultimately, the process of spiritual growth depends on our openness to the movement of God. These twenty traits, therefore, are not meant to be some sort of a checklist. Rather, they are intended to point to some of the ways God is alive and active in our very real lives.

We are almost ready to look at our first trait of a healthy spirituality. But before we do that, we must take a look at that important word: spirituality.

Spirituality

Where Are You?

Spirituality is meeting God in all that life is.
—Patricia Livingston

Spirituality is the experience of integrating self-transcendence within the horizon of ultimacy. —Sandra Schneiders

Spirituality is how I cope with life. —Gerard Broccolo

An old recipe for rabbit stew begins with this directive: "Catch rabbit." Obviously the person who wrote the recipe was taking nothing for granted. In writing this book, I wish to take nothing for granted either. That's why, as I begin it, I am following this directive: "define spirituality." For it stands to reason that before we can look at the traits of a *healthy* spirituality we must first know what we mean by *spirituality*.

The word spirituality has been defined in many ways. Historically, spirituality was often equated with the so-called religious aspects of the Christian life such as prayer, penance, and fasting. More recently the word has been defined in broader terms. In one sense, Christian spirituality is synonymous with Christian living. As theology professor Michael Downey says, "Spirituality is not merely an aspect of Christian life, it is the Christian life lived in response to the Spirit."

Traditionally, spirituality stressed our relationship with God. More recently the word calls attention to other relationships as

4

well. Gerard Broccolo, in his book *Vital Spiritualities*, subscribes to this broader view when he writes: "Spirituality...involves a way of viewing and experiencing God, self, others, and the world." Today we also emphasize the fact that our spirituality can never be divorced from the time and place in which we live. Dyckman and Carroll make this point clear in their book *Inviting the Mystic, Supporting the Prophet:* "Spirituality is the style of a person's response to Christ before the challenge of everyday life, in a given historical and cultural environment."

Spirituality as Our Outlook on Life

The owner of a priceless antiques collection was allowing a museum to exhibit some of his valuable treasures. While the movers packed his vases, the owner hovered nervously over them. To one burly mover, the man cautioned, "Please be careful with that vase. It's nearly two thousand years old!" The mover replied, "Don't worry, Mister. I'll treat it like it was brand new!"

The story illustrates the fact that individuals can view things in very different ways. I like to think of spirituality in those terms: it is the way we view things. More specifically spirituality is *our basic outlook on life.* St. Paul exhorts us to "Let the same *mind* be in you that was in Christ Jesus" (Phil 2:5). Spirituality, then, is our endeavor to perceive reality more and more with the mind (and heart) of Jesus. This means all of reality and not simply the so-called religious aspects of our life. Our spirituality colors the way we look at everything—from ourselves to others, from God to the stock market, from love to platypuses.

But spirituality goes beyond the mere perception of reality. It also includes our *responses* to reality, that is, the actions and behaviors that flow from that perception. Our spirituality is expressed in the little daily decisions and choices we make: what kind of food we eat, how we talk to the clerk in the store, how much time (if any) we devote to prayer. Our spirituality also includes the big choices we make: whom we decide to marry or befriend, the kind of home we live in, the type of work we choose to do. When life presents us with few options, our spirituality influences the way we accept and work within the confines of such restrictions. When life gives us no choice at all, our spirituality determines the way we deal with such "givens," the way we face the inevitable.

Christian spirituality is not something reserved for Sundays or Christmas Eve. It is lived every day—including rainy Mondays and ordinary days in the middle of February. Our spirituality is reflected in how we do the so-called holy things in life—such as pray to God, give alms to the poor, and forgive those who have wronged us. But it is also shown in how we do the so-called ordinary things—such as eat an apple, stand in a checkout line, greet a stranger, notice a robin. As author Joann Wolski Conn says, "Spirituality includes every dimension of human life."

Spirituality: One, Unique, and Ongoing

Christian spirituality has three characteristics: it is *one*, it is *unique*, it is *ongoing*. Christian spirituality is one. This means it has certain "constants" or certain universal traits. For example, Christian spirituality has its foundations in the death and resurrection of Jesus. Any spirituality claiming to be Christian, then, must be rooted in the paschal mystery. Other constants of Christian spirituality would include things like the primacy of love, the mandate of forgiveness, the necessity of prayer.

Christian spirituality is, at the same time, unique. No two individuals have exactly the same perspective on life. Each of us sees life differently, depending on our genetic makeup, our past experiences, our gender and age, our educational background, etc. Just as our perspective on life is unique to each one of us, so too is our spirituality—as unique as our fingerprints or DNA. Even though we may share many beliefs and practices with other Christians, none of us has a "spiritual clone."

Christian spirituality is also ongoing. It is always in process. This means we can never say our spirituality is fully formed or finished. We always have more things to learn and more ways to grow. God is forever calling us to greater conversion. (The very fact that you are taking the time to read this book is a pretty good sign that you believe spirituality is ongoing.)

God Asks: "Where Are You?"

There is an incident in the book of Genesis that reminds us how God is forever calling us to greater conversion. Adam and Eve had just disobeyed God by eating fruit from the Tree of Knowledge. Later that day, when God came to the garden in the cool of the evening to walk with them, Adam and Eve were ashamed of their sin and hid themselves among the trees. God called out to them and asked, "Where are you?" (cf. Gn 3:8–9)

In reflecting on this incident, someone has posed the question: "Because God is all-knowing, God certainly knew what Adam and Eve had done and where they were hiding. Why then did God ask them, 'Where are you?'" Judaic philosopher Martin Buber provides a good answer. He says God asked Adam and Eve that question not to learn something new. Rather, God asked that question in order to make Adam and Eve confront their current state in life. When God asked them, "Where are you?" God was really asking them, "Where are you—in relationship to me, to yourself, to each other, to your world? How far along are you on your journey?"

God asks us the same question today. "Where are you?" God asks it not to learn something new, but rather, as author Wilkie Au expresses it, God asks it "to jolt us into examining our lives and taking responsibility for our way of living." God is asking us today, "Where are you? How far along are you in your Christian journey?" Hopefully the following chapters will help us to answer that question.

Questions for Reflection

1. Read the three definitions of spirituality found at the beginning of this chapter. Which one do you like best or least? Why?

2. How would you define spirituality?

3. What are some of the factors that have contributed to your own spirituality?

4. Why are you reading this book?

Practice

I will hear God ask me this question today: "Where are you?" And I will tell God where I am.

You Ask Me, "Where are you?"

God, you ask me,
"Where are you?"
And I reply,
"What need have I to tell you where I am,
when you, who know the whole of life,
know better where I am than I?"
And you reply, "That's true. I do."
But then you add,
"But do *you* know where you are?"
And I confess, "I don't."
And quickly add:
"I think I hide from you and from myself,
with all the things I have to do
or choose to do.
And things can sometimes stand between
the who I am and the who I want to be,
and the who you want me to be."
"You're right," you say.
And then it all comes clear to me,
what I must do to become the who
we both want me to be:
I must walk with you and talk with you,
in the warmth of the morning sun,
or in the cool of evening breezes.
God, when you ask, "Where are you?"
May my answer always be:
"With you, my God. With you."
Amen.

Self-Esteem

We Are Saints and Sinners

You have to start knowing yourself so well that you begin to know other people. A piece of us is in every person we can ever meet.
— John D. MacDonald

You have no idea what a poor opinion I have of myself, and how little I deserve it!
—W. S. Gilbert

Every new adjustment is a crisis in self-esteem.
—Eric Hoffer

One warm summer day I was in the backyard of a convent in Sheffield Lake, Ohio, sitting in the sun gazing out over the beautiful blue waters of Lake Erie. Suddenly I felt something brushing against my legs. Startled, I looked down and saw a huge tomcat. Even though I like cats, I lifted my feet up onto the chair, for this particular cat was dirty, ugly, and mean-looking. His grayish brown fur was in clumps, his right ear was almost chewed off, and his tail had a forty-five-degree bend in it. I concluded that here was a tomcat who had seen considerable combat.

Despite my cold reception, the cat didn't go away. In fact, he began rubbing himself against the legs of my chair while looking up at me and meowing in a deep baritone voice. Notwithstanding his mangy appearance, the cat was genuinely friendly. Cautiously I reached down to pet him. He willingly gave himself over to my hand. Within minutes he was on his back and I was stroking him under his chin while he purred with contentment.

I remember saying to that cat, "You have one of the healthiest self-concepts I have ever seen!" It was true. For there he was, old, mean-looking, and as ugly as sin, yet he was confidently reaching out to me for affection. So in touch was he with his own goodness (so intact was his self-esteem!), that he knew I, too, would eventually find him lovable—once I saw beneath the surface. (And I did!) I think of that wonderful cat every time I reflect on self-esteem—which is, by the way, our first trait of a healthy spirituality.

Self-knowledge

Let us begin our exploration of self-esteem with a few words about self-knowledge. It was Socrates who uttered that famous dictum: "Know thyself." He was implying, of course, that all real knowledge begins with self-knowledge. Or, to paraphrase another popular proverb, "Knowledge (like charity) begins at home." In one way, we can say that all self-esteem begins with self-knowledge.

Jesus knew the importance of self-knowledge. His famous injunction, "Do to others as you would have them do to you" (Lk 6:31), presupposes self-knowledge: we must know ourselves well enough to know how we would like to be treated before we can treat others in a similar way. On several occasions Jesus directed his listeners' attention inward. He warns them to "consider whether the light in you is not darkness" (Lk 11:35). Another time he chided certain individuals for their lack of self-knowledge: "Why do you see the speck in your neighbor's eye, but do not notice the log in your own eye?" (Mt 7:3)

Jesus also knew the importance of self-esteem. He directed his followers to "love your neighbor as yourself" (Mk 12:31). Too often we concentrate only on the first part of that great commandment: love your neighbor. We sometimes gloss over the second part which is just as important: as yourself. Jesus was implying that a certain amount of love of self is not only permissible for Christian living, it is downright essential. How can we begin to see the goodness in others if we haven't taken the time to notice the goodness in ourselves?

In his book *One Minute Wisdom*, Anthony De Mello, SJ, presents a short dialogue between a spiritual master and his student:

"Why don't I see goodness and beauty everywhere?" the student asks.

The master replies, "Because you cannot see outside of you what you fail to see inside."

Self-Esteem

What exactly is self-esteem? The following dialogue tells us in a humorous way:

Woman:	"Did anyone ever tell you what a terrific, talented, handsome guy you are?"
Man (smiling):	"Why no, I don't think anyone ever did."
Woman:	"Then where did you ever get the idea?"

Self-esteem is the idea we get of ourselves. Or, as William Appleton puts it, self-esteem is the "reputation" we have with ourselves. Self-esteem is grounded in the image we have of who we are. How do we get our self-image? We begin to get it even while we are small children. Our parents or those individuals who raise us play a key role in shaping that early image we have of ourselves. If we see acceptance in their eyes, we will sense that we are lovable. If we encounter rejection, we will feel unlovable. Later on, siblings, friends, and teachers play important roles in influencing our self-image.

This self-image, however, is not determined solely by others. We ourselves contribute significantly to the concept we have of ourselves. What we think of ourselves depends largely on how we interpret the many messages we receive from other people and from the many happenings in our lives. If someone fails to greet us in a congested hallway at work, for example, how do we interpret that? Do we say, "He probably didn't see me, that's all"? Or do we think, "He's mad at me—I just know it"? If we fail to achieve some personal goal, do we say, "I feel bad" or "I'm no good"? The way we translate the messages life sends us has a lot to do with who we think we are.

I maintain that self-esteem is a very fragile thing—something like a crocus in February or a snowflake in May. My experience has been that even seemingly confident and successful individuals possess a fragile self-esteem. I know a highly successful college professor, for example, who has a national reputation for excellence in his field and who is extremely popular with his students. Yet he told me how even one negative comment by a single student in just one of his classes can haunt him for days. I was happy that he knew this about himself (self-knowledge is very important, remember), but I was even happier that he could share this with me. I confessed to him, "It's the same with me and my writing. If I get ten letters of enthusiastic praise and one letter of negative criticism, guess which one I remember for days?" He guessed rightly. The point is that many of us seem programmed to dismiss the positive messages we receive about ourselves and to exaggerate the negative ones. Acknowledging this can be the first step toward doing something about it.

Self-Esteem and Our Christian Faith

Our Christian faith provides us with valuable insights with regard to self-esteem. First of all, our faith, at its best, presents us with a remarkably balanced view of the human person. It tells us that we are both saint and sinner. The Bible affirms our goodness. In Genesis we read, "God saw everything that he had made, and indeed, it was very good" (Gn 1:31). The popular poster echoes this fundamental belief: "God made me—and God don't make junk!" In addition, Genesis tells us that we are made in the image and likeness of God. What further proof do we need of our basic goodness? The psalms, too, celebrate the dignity of the human person: "Yet you have made them a little lower than God, and crowned them with glory and honor" (Ps 8:5).

When Jesus came, he continued to remind us of our inherent worth. He told us we were sons and daughters of God. He called us his friends, his brothers and sisters. He demonstrated just how much he loved us by suffering and dying on the cross for us. If we really believe that Jesus loves us, how could we ever think of ourselves as worthless? As William Larkin tells us in his book *Get Real*

About Yourself, "The love of Christ...is the root of all self-esteem."

But our faith also teaches us that, despite our innate goodness, we can and do commit evil. We are not only saints, we are sinners. People with a healthy self-concept, then, are in touch with both aspects of themselves: saint and sinner. They know their assets as well as their liabilities, their strengths as well as their weaknesses. Such individuals have a keen awareness of their own sin. They know the evil they recoil from in others is lurking within their own hearts.

In his book *Care of the Soul,* Thomas Moore reminds us how important it is for us to be aware of our own capacity to do evil. Using the example of violence he writes, "We only sustain violence in our world if we fail to admit its place in our own hearts and identify only with unaffecting innocence." That was precisely what the Pharisees did and what Jesus condemned with so much passion. The Pharisees identified solely with innocence. They failed to see the sin in their own hearts. If we have a healthy spirituality, we will have a healthy self-concept. It's as simple (and as difficult) as that. This means we will never forget our basic goodness—no matter what terrible things we may have done. We are always a child of God or, as the old church hymn says, "We always have a friend in Jesus." At the same time, we must never underestimate our own capacity to do evil. Like the publican in Jesus' parable, we must never forget to pray, "Have mercy on me, a sinner."

There is a story of an old rabbi who prayed to God, "O Lord, make me holy! Make me like Moses!" But God replied to him, "What need have I of another Moses? I already have one! But what I really could use is you!" One definitive sign of a healthy spirituality is if we can say, "I'm happy I'm me!" and if we can believe, "God is happy I'm me too!"

Questions for Reflection

1. Read the three quotations at the beginning of this chapter. How do they strike you?

2. If self-knowledge is so important in our spiritual life, what are some practical ways we can grow in self-knowledge?

3. Do you agree or disagree that self-esteem is fragile? Why or why not?

4. Is there anything else that was said about self-esteem in this chapter that resonates with you and your experience? If so, what and why?

Practice
I will draw up a list of my strengths and weaknesses, my assets and liabilities, and talk them over with God.

Between Dust and Angelhood
Dear God,
    your Bible says it well:
    what a work we humans are!
In one sense: "mere dust of the earth";
    in another: "little less than the angels."
At times, God,
    I feel that pull inside
    between dust and angelhood.
Help me to grow in self-knowledge
    by giving me the courage to look inside.
May I have a healthy self-esteem,
    one that steers clear
    of demonic despair
    and Pharisaic pride.
May I never identify solely with innocence.
Rather, help me to know my sins and failings
    while never doubting
    the flow of your mercy.
God, source of all esteem,
    help me to say each day,
    "I'm happy I'm me."
And to hear you reply,
    "Me too!"
Amen.

W<u>onde</u>R

Sitting on God's Front Porch

I did not ask for success; I asked for wonder.
—Abraham Heschel

We should not spend all our time standing over above or over against the world. We should spend as much time as possible in wonder and appreciation, looking up. —Miriam Pollard

It is nice to think how one can be recklessly lost in a daisy.
—Anne Morrow Lindbergh

Albert Einstein once said, "One who can no longer pause to wonder and stand rapt in awe is as good as dead." Perhaps we can also say, "If we can no longer pause to wonder and stand rapt in awe, our spirituality is dead too!" For there is a definite link between having a sense of wonder and living the Christian faith—so much so that it's fairly safe to say that a sense of wonder is another trait of a healthy spirituality.

St. Thomas Aquinas would agree, for he also saw a correlation between wonder and faith. Aquinas wrote that a sense of wonder "sets a person's feet on the ladder that leads up to the beatific vision." In other words, wonder is often the prelude to meeting God. It is, so to speak, like sitting on the front porch of God's house.

Why is a sense of wonder a trait of a healthy spirituality? For one thing, when we wonder about things we are acknowledging that some things are clearly beyond our understanding. We don't know everything there is to know—far from it—no matter how brilliant, educated, or experienced we may be. How, for example, did the universe come to be? What drives the salmon to return to their place of origin in order to spawn? Why do we humans do some of the silly, heroic, or terrible things that we do? We may speculate about these mysteries and even come up with some plausible theories, but the truth remains: we know very few things for sure. In fact, the more we know, the more we know we don't know.

This fact does not have to overwhelm or depress us. On the contrary, genuine wonder can fascinate us and spur us on to further investigation. Wilbur and Orville Wright's fascination with the mystery of flight, for example, eventually brought them to that sand dune at Kitty Hawk. Wonder is the first cousin to religious awe. Abraham Heschel defines awe as "an intuition for the dignity of all things (which) enables us to perceive in the world intimations of the divine." Wonder encourages us to stand humbly before the unfathomable mysteries of human life, trusting that, in them, we encounter God.

Wonder in Scripture

Scripture reminds us how wonder can lead to a meeting with divinity. Take, for example, the story of Moses and his encounter with God in the burning bush. We are probably familiar with the Exodus narrative (3:1–17). Moses was tending his father-in-law's sheep on a hillside one day, when he suddenly noticed something unusual: a bush that seemed to be on fire without being burned up. "That's strange," Moses said to himself, and he decided to go and have a closer look at the bush. As he drew near, the voice of God called out to him from the bush, "Moses! Moses!" Eventually God commissioned Moses to lead the Israelites from their bondage in Egypt to the freedom of the promised land. In addition, God revealed to Moses God's name, "I am who am," a gesture of hitherto unheard-of intimacy on God's part.

We might ask ourselves: What would have happened if Moses had not noticed the bush in the first place? What if he had been so preoccupied with his work that he never even saw the bush? Or what if he saw it but felt he couldn't afford to take the time to go and have a closer look? The answer is both clear and sobering: Moses would have missed an opportunity to meet God.

Scripture is filled with examples of other individuals whose sense of wonder eventually led them to God. The first apostles were so intrigued with Jesus that they left their boats and nets to follow him. Zacchaeus was so curious about Jesus that he climbed a tree in order to get a glimpse of him. The woman at the well was so captivated by Jesus that she not only gave him water to drink, she stayed for quite some time to converse with him.

Jesus, too, gives ample evidence of a keen sense of wonder. As a young boy, he was so enchanted by the teachers in the temple at Jerusalem that he stayed behind to listen and converse with them. As an adult, Jesus marveled at life—all of life. He stood in wonder before the birds of the air, the lilies of the field, and the gathering of storm clouds. He was fascinated by bread rising, wheat ripening, and wine aging. Jesus marveled at people too. He marveled at the incredible compassion of a Roman centurion, the unbelievable faith of a Syro-Phoenician woman, and the thoughtful gratitude of a freshly cured leper. Jesus could face even the mystery of his own passion with unfaltering trust in God, believing completely that even the power of death is nothing compared to the wonder of God's love.

Growing in Wonder

If wonder plays such an important role in our spiritual lives, as scripture seems to testify, what are some of the attitudes we must guard against that can stifle or even extinguish our sense of wonder? Although there are a number of them, let's look at three.

We think we know it all. Nothing kills a sense of wonder more quickly than a know-it-all attitude. This attitude is expressed in thoughts or comments such as these: "If there's one thing I know completely, it's my religion." "Once you've seen one, you've seen them all." (That word "one" could refer to anything—one woman, one teenager, one priest, one lawyer, one daisy, one sparrow, etc.) "Living has no surprises for me any more." On the other hand, comments such as the following often indicate the presence of a healthy sense of wonder: "I'm always learning new things about my Christian faith." "No two individuals are exactly alike." Or a simple, "Wow! That's neat!"

We are too preoccupied or too busy to pay attention to things. Someone has said, "Attention makes the genius; all learning, fancy, science, and skill depend upon it." Similarly we can say, "Attention makes the wonderer. A sense of wonder depends on it." So another attitude that stifles wonder is being too preoccupied or too busy to pay attention to things. As was noted earlier, Moses was busy tending his sheep, yet he took time to pay attention to the burning bush. The first apostles had to lay aside their nets in order to spend time with Jesus. Zacchaeus stopped collecting taxes long enough to climb that tree. The lesson is clear: our sense of wonder is nourished by periodically laying aside our preoccupations and our work in order to pay closer attention to our world and the people around us. This means doing things like spending time with loved ones, pausing to reassess our priorities, stopping to watch a sunset, making time for prayer.

We feel fear and mistrust. A third attitude that chokes wonder is one of fear and mistrust. Moses could have been frightened by the burning bush and run away from it. Instead, he overcame whatever fear he might have had and walked toward it. The woman at the well displayed considerable courage when she engaged in conversation with Jesus in public. Zacchaeus, too, showed great trust in Jesus when he eagerly welcomed him into his home.

In his book *The Spirit Master*, John Shea writes: "The richness and variety of life offer us astonishment at every turn. The human situation is being modified in the direction of redemption daily. We are witness to this."

Could anything be more wonderful?

Questions for Reflection

1. Read the three quotations at the beginning of this chapter. What does each one say to you personally?

2. Have you ever had an experience of wonder which led to some kind of an encounter with God?

3. What are some things that stifle your sense of wonder? What

can you do about them?

4. Think of someone you know who has a sense of wonder. In what ways does this individual give evidence of a sense of wonder?

Practice

I will take time to pay attention to just one aspect of the "richness and variety of life" today and talk to God about what I see.

I Ask for Wonder

Dear God,
    I ask for wonder.
The kind of wonder that looks
    not down at or against,
    but up to and for.
The kind that sets my feet
    on the ladder that leads to you.
Give me wonder to perceive
    the dignity of all things,
    and to glimpse in creation
    the intimations of your own goodness.
Let me never think I know it all
    or even most of all there is to know.
May "Wow! That's neat!"
    be often on my lips.
God, help me to *make* time
    to stop and take a closer look
    at everything around and inside of me,
    trusting you so much
    I can risk exploring
    all the burning bushes
    of my everyday world.
Dear God, I ask for wonder
    for I believe all wonder
    is but a prelude to meeting you.
Amen.

Friendship

The "You Too?" Experience

*Those who would take friendship out of life would seem to take the
sun out of the world.*   —Cicero

*For those who live in the world and desire to embrace true virtue,
it is necessary to unite together in holy, sacred friendship.*
                                                    —St. Francis de Sales

God is friendship.   —St. Aelred of Rievaulx

The old proverb says, "Tell me who your friends are, and I will tell
you who you are." We could just as easily say, "Tell me who your
friends are, and I will tell you what your spirituality is." For another sign of a healthy spirituality is this: we have friends, good
friends.

In his book *The Four Loves*, C.S. Lewis devotes an entire chapter
to a discussion of friendship, describing in detail how most friendships begin. A group of individuals find themselves together "talking shop," writes Lewis. He calls this kind of coming together
"companionship" or "clubbableness," and, although this is not in
itself friendship, it can lead to friendship. Friendship begins when
two or more of these individuals discover that they have something in common—what Lewis describes as "some insight or interest or even taste which the others do not share and which, till that
moment, each believed to be his own unique treasure (or bur-

den)." Friendship is born when one of the individuals says something like, "What? You too? I thought I was the only one."

According to Lewis, all friendship arises from this "You Too?" experience. It is born the instant we detect that another individual shares something of our own vision of life, that is, when we realize that this other person sees the same truth we see (as Ralph Waldo Emerson puts it) or at least cares about the same truth (as Lewis puts it).

What Good Friends Do for Us

I began this chapter by saying that one trait of a healthy spirituality is having good friends. That word *good* is important. Anyone can have friends. Even a man like Adolf Hitler had friends and yet no one would ever accuse him of having a healthy spirituality! But *good* friends are much more than just friends. Good friends are good because they help us to be better people.

I can think of about five different ways in which friends help us to grow. First, they help us to grow in self-knowledge—and we already saw how important that is for our spiritual life. As James Schall, SJ, said, "The discovery of who we are is ultimately bound up with the discovery of another person." In other words, in friendship we discover not only things about our friend, we discover things about ourselves by relating to that friend. We grow in self-knowledge by learning what we have in common with our friend: we both like to go for walks, for example, or we both enjoy Chinese food, or we both like jazz or hockey. But we also discover who we are by coming to know the ways we are different from our friend: he devours murder mysteries while I sip on nineteenth-century British poetry; she's a night owl while I'm an early bird; he prays best late in the evening while I pray best early in the morning.

I said earlier that spirituality is our basic outlook on life. Another way good friends help us is by expanding that outlook. My friend, for example, urges me to read a murder mystery and I learn that I enjoy this type of book. Or my friend convinces me to go white water rafting—something I never would have done on my own—and I have a fun time. Or my friend suggests I try a new way of praying and, doing so, I find my prayer life enriched.

A third way good friends help us is by giving us encouragement. In his book *Touching the Holy*, Robert Wicks tells how important such encouragement can be. To live in today's stressful and complex world "without the presence of solidly supportive friends is foolhardy and dangerous," Wicks says. "Warm friends represent the incarnational love of God in our lives," he concludes. Friends also represent the unconditional love of God for us. Our friends, while encouraging us in our efforts to do good, also love and embrace us—warts, foibles, and all.

Good friends also help us by allowing us to love them back. This means that friends afford us the opportunity to express our love in specific and concrete ways—for example, by giving them a hug, by patting them on the back, by listening to them, by sharing their excitement, by consoling them in their grief. Good friends are forever reminding us what it means to love and to be loved by God. In this regard we can paraphrase those beautiful words of St. John and say, "How can you claim to be friends with God whom you cannot see, if you don't have friends whom you can see!"

And lastly, friends help us to grow in our ability to trust. With good friends we find ourselves sharing everything—our hopes and dreams, our fears and misgivings, our accomplishments and disappointments—trusting that our friends understand us and love us no matter what. In his book *The Friendship Game*, Andrew Greeley says that one of the critical problems in today's world is the absence of trust. He concludes, people "cannot trust because they do not have enough friendship in their life. If there were more friendships in the world there would be more trust."

Making Ourselves More Friendable

If friendship is so important in today's world, then how can we make ourselves more "friendable"? American writer and publisher Elbert Hubbard gives us this simple recipe for having friends: "Be one." I would like to suggest three ways we might do this.

First we can become more "clubbable," to use Lewis' word. By this I mean we can mingle more with other people and thus give friendship a chance to be born. We won't make friends sitting by ourselves. We first have to get in touch with other people—whether in person, on the phone, through the mail, or even through the Internet. A second way we make ourselves more friendable is by developing our ability to listen. If we spend our time with others talking only about ourselves, friendship has little chance of blooming. If, on the other hand, we can invite others to share something of themselves—perhaps through asking a few simple questions—friendship just might blossom in our lives.

A third way we become more friendable is by becoming a more interesting and upbeat person. This means we take a real interest in the larger world and not just our own little corner of it. We read, we ask questions, we learn, we try new things, we keep our curiosity alive. After all, interested people make the most interesting friends. And upbeat people are more apt to have friends than sourpusses.

Jesus and Friendship

Jesus had friends. In fact, one of the outstanding characteristics of Jesus' life and ministry was his ability to befriend people. With only a few words, he won over the hearts of those burly fisherman on the shores of the Sea of Galilee, he convinced the tax collector Matthew to walk away from the customs house forever, and he coaxed the outcast Zacchaeus down from the security of that sycamore tree.

The gospels show Jesus frequently engaged in conversation with a variety of individuals: a Roman centurion, a synagogue official, a blind man, the woman at the well. Jesus listened well to others and often asked questions that encouraged them to share their thoughts and feelings with him. Jesus also frequently ate with his friends and enjoyed spending time in their company. In fact, so often did he dine with others that his enemies labeled him a glutton.

On more than one occasion Jesus took his closest friends, the twelve apostles, aside for some R&R together. Shortly before his death he returned one last time to Bethany to spend quality time with Lazarus, Mary, and Martha, three of his dearest friends. At the last supper Jesus said these beautiful words to all present,

"You are my friends" (Jn 15:14). During his agony in the garden, he unashamedly sought support and consolation from three special friends, Peter, James, and John. Even when most of his friends deserted him during his trial and crucifixion, Jesus did not give up on friendship. Instead, after his resurrection, he gave friendship another chance by forgiving those friends who had deserted him.

Having good friends is a vital aspect of our Christian spirituality. Writer Eugene Kennedy goes so far as to say that the ability to share friendship with others "is the distinguishing mark of the Christian." Little wonder C.S. Lewis could say with such conviction, "Friendship has been by far the chief source of my happiness."

Questions for Reflection
1. Read the three quotations at the beginning of this chapter. Which one speaks to you the most and why?

2. Have you ever had a "You too?" experience with someone? If so, describe how it came about.

3. Reflect on someone you consider a good friend. In what ways has this individual helped you in your life?

4. Can you think of other factors that make a person more "friendable" besides the ones given here? How friendable are you?

Practice
I will reach out in friendship to someone today.

Thank You for Good Friends
Dear God,
    thank you for good friends.
Thank you for those times
    I've said "You too?" to someone
    as I suddenly discovered
    that someone else shares with me
    some insight, interest, or taste.
That someone else
    sees the same truth I see

or at least cares about the same truth.
Thank you for the ways my friends
    help me to discover who I am
    and expand my outlook on life.
The way they give me encouragement
    and incarnate your unconditional love for me.
God, help me to love my friends
    as you love me,
    with patience, sensitivity, and trust.
I ask for these things
    through Jesus, your son,
    remembering well
    that on the night before
    he gave his life for us,
    he called us
    friends.
Amen.

Courage

When God Comes as Earthquake

Smooth seas do not make skillful sailors.   —African proverb

No one comes to heaven with dry eyes.   —Anonymous

Often a long, dark night of the soul is the door through which we find the Promised Land, the living water, the encounter with God.
                                                    —Christine Gudorf

---

M. Scott Peck, MD, begins his best-selling book, *The Road Less Traveled,* with the words "Life is difficult." He goes on to explain that problems arise when we forget this great truth, when we moan and groan and complain about the enormity of our problems as if life *were* easy or *should* be easy.

A healthy spirituality does not deny the fact that life is difficult. It does not gloss over the very real challenges and pains of everyday life, nor does it provide us with immediate and simple solutions to problems that are long-standing and complex. Rather, a healthy spirituality helps us to name life's problems and pains, to face them squarely, to work untiringly toward solving or eradicating them, and, when this is not possible (at least for now) to endure them with courage.

The Many Faces of Adversity
Adversity has many faces. The following true anecdote illustrates this fact. A wallpaper hanger was hanging paper in a suite

of offices. When a piece of paper failed to stick, he let out a string of expletives. Suddenly realizing that a computer operator in the office overheard him, he said to her apologetically, "I'm sorry. That's paper-hanging talk." She replied, "Don't worry, honey. It's computer talk too!"

We all meet adversity—whether we're hanging wallpaper, using a computer, baking brownies, or petting a puppy. Simply put, adversity is not getting our way. It is not having things turn out the way we would like them to turn out. The wallpaper doesn't stick, the computer doesn't follow our commands, the brownies get burned, the puppy wets all over our shoe. That's adversity. It's something we know from the day we are born and are thrust from the warm, dark, quiet of our mother's womb out into the cold, glaring, noisy world. Immediately we protest this first experience of adversity in the only way we know how: by crying our little heads off.

As we grow into childhood, we experience other forms of adversity: the discomfort of a wet diaper, the bitter taste of brussels sprouts, a "D" on a test. As we become adults, adversity takes more sophisticated forms such as conflicts within our family, misunderstandings with friends, tensions at work, personal disappointments.

Life presents us with both major adversities and lesser ones. Major adversities include things like the death of a spouse, marital problems, personal injury or ill health, the loss of a job, major financial difficulties. As serious as these hardships may be, we must not overlook those lesser but very real irritations we encounter almost every day: headaches, sore joints, traffic jams, noise, lack of time, misplaced articles, waiting in line, fear of crime, and worry about the future. Psychologists tell us that, over a period of time, these little hassles of daily life can do just as much damage, or even more damage, than the major difficulties we experience.

When God Comes as Earthquake

A healthy spirituality helps us to see the connection between the adversities we encounter and the presence of God in our lives.

This is not to say that God directly puts adversities into our lives. If we are honest, we will realize that most of the difficulties we experience in life are simply the result of the human condition. None of us is perfect. Through our sin and selfishness, we cause each other considerable pain and sorrow.

But the fact remains that too often Christian spirituality mistakenly identifies the presence of God solely with peace and tranquillity. In the Book of Kings, for example, when the prophet Elijah encounters God in a cave, God appears in the form of a gentle breeze. Similarly, spiritual writers over the centuries often equated God's presence with the feeling of peace. Even at Mass today we pray to be freed from all anxiety—as if anxiety were bad and should be eradicated. (I know a priest who, firmly believing that anxiety is not always bad, says we should ask God at Mass to free us from all *needless* anxiety.)

A well-known anecdote in the life of St. Teresa of Avila sheds some light on the relationship between God and adversity. Teresa, no stranger to adversity, once complained to God about all the troubles God seemed to be sending into her life. God said to her, "That's the way I treat all my friends." To which the spunky saint replied, "Then no wonder you have so few!" The story, though humorous, makes a serious point: even though God may not be directly responsible for the difficulties we're experiencing in life, God is nonetheless with us as we deal with them. As Paul Claudel writes, "Jesus came not to eradicate suffering, but to fill it with his presence."

A Hasidic teaching supports the claim that God can be found in adversity. It says, "God is an earthquake," reminding us that, although God can sometimes come into our life as a gentle breeze, God can just as often come as an earthquake.

Mary of Nazareth

We can find no better example of God's coming as an earthquake into someone's life than in the story of Jesus' own mother, Mary of Nazareth. We first meet her in the Gospel of Luke in the story of the Annunciation (Lk 1:26–38). When we read this account, we must remind ourselves that Mary was a real human being. She was not a person sitting around waiting for an angel to show up and tell her what to do next. No, she, like us, was living an ordinary life which included making decisions. Mary had plans—the most obvious was her plan to marry Joseph. But then God, through Gabriel, suddenly barged into her life with a seemingly outrageous proposal. God asked Mary to conceive and bear a child, the Son of the most high God. Mary was puzzled and asked, "How can this be since I do not know man?" Her question showed she instinctively knew how earth-shaking God's proposal was. But once Gabriel explained how the conception and birth would come about, Mary said those magnificent words, "I am the handmaid of the Lord. Be it done unto me according to your word." A young girl said "yes" to an angel and God became incarnate on our planet.

After saying her yes, Mary encountered one adversity after another. Her pregnancy jeopardized her relationship with Joseph, a man she loved. By saying "yes" to God, Mary put her reputation and life on the line; for in those days, an unfaithful woman was ordinarily stoned to death. The birth of Mary's son was fraught with hardships: the journey to Bethlehem during her ninth month of pregnancy; the birth in a cold, dark, smelly stable; the flight into Egypt, a foreign country. Later on Mary suffered misunderstandings with her twelve-year-old son in the temple. Years later, after Jesus began his public ministry, she witnessed the rise of his popularity and his subsequent notoriety. When she got word of his arrest, she went to Jerusalem and stood by the cross while he was executed as a common criminal. If God permitted the mother of Jesus to suffer in this way, then should we be surprised when we also encounter hardships in life?

God Shouts to Us in Our Pain

A few years ago I read a book entitled *When Bad Things Happen to Good People,* in which author Harold Kushner attempted to answer the age-old question: why does God allow people to suffer—especially good people? The truth is, no one knows for sure the answer to that question. Suffering is one of life's greatest mysteries. Yet, even with our limited vision, we sometimes catch glimpses of the good that comes from our struggles.

German theologian Meister Eckhart called adversity "the aptitude for sensitivity." Adversity, in this sense, can make us more sensitive, more compassionate. It is probably true that the most sensitive doctors and nurses are those who have had some experience of ill health along the way. Similarly, the best teachers are often those who struggled as students at some point during their schooling. Besides making us more compassionate, adversity can also make us more humble—especially when we deal with problems that won't go away despite our best efforts. As we struggle with our own bad habits and compulsive behaviors, for example, or as we try again and again to be more patient, more honest, more kind, we come to realize this great truth: we cannot go it alone in life. Adversity can make us realize just how much we need God's help—a realization absolutely essential for spiritual growth.

In summary, then, one sign of a healthy spirituality is our ability to live with adversity, knowing that it is often through our difficulties and pain that we hear God most clearly. As C. S. Lewis said so well, "God whispers to us in our pleasures, speaks in our conscience, but shouts in our pains."

Questions for Reflection

1. Read the three quotations at the beginning of this chapter and decide if you agree or disagree with them.

2. What are some of the minor adversities that you find difficult? What helps you to endure them?

3. Reflect on a major struggle you experienced in the past. What helped you to face this trial or struggle? Were you able to see any good that came from this experience of adversity? If so, what?

4. Can you think of someone that exemplifies courage for you? If so, in what way do they do this?

Practice

I will share with God the struggles and pains I'm experiencing today and ask God to speak to me through them.

Life is Difficult

Dear God,
 life is difficult.
Help me to realize this great truth
 and not moan and groan
 and complain about my problems
 as if life were easy or should be easy.
Teach me to name my real problems,
 to face them squarely,
 and to work untiringly toward solving them,
 or, if this is not possible,
 then to endure them with courage.
Help me to be open to all the ways
 you come into my life:
 whether as gentle breeze,
 tumultuous earthquake,
 or something in between.
May the difficulties I experience
 bear only good fruit:
 sensitivity, compassion,
 patience, humility,
 and the growing realization
 of my absolute need for you.
God, I ask for all these things
 through Jesus
 and the gentle,
 yet earth-shaking
 power of the Spirit.
Amen.

Teachability

Prerequisite for Conversion

The best thing for being sad, replied Merlin..., is to learn some-thing. —Terence H. White

The question to ask is not whether you are a success or a failure, but whether you are a learner or a nonlearner. —Benjamin Barber

Fall seven times, stand up eight. —Japanese proverb

On his fifty-first birthday, H. Jackson Brown decided to jot down some of the lessons he had learned during his lifetime. He wrote down the phrase "I've learned that..." twenty times on a piece of paper and proceeded to complete the sentences. So enjoyable was the exercise for him, that Brown began asking his friends and acquaintances to do the same thing. Eventually he enlisted the help of hundreds of other people from kindergarten kids to senior citizens. The result is his fascinating little book called *Live and Learn and Pass It On*, a compilation of what hundreds of individuals say they have learned from life. Here are a few examples:

"I've learned that trust is the single most important factor in both personal and professional relationships" (age twenty).

"I've learned that even when I have pains, I don't have to be a pain" (age eighty-two).

"I've learned that you can't hug your kids too much" (age fifty-four).

"I've learned that you can tell a lot about a man by the way he handles these three things: a rainy holiday, lost luggage, and tangled Christmas tree lights" (age fifty-two).

"I've learned that you can't hide a piece of broccoli in a glass of milk" (age seven).

Brown's delightful book reminds us of yet another trait of a healthy spirituality: the ability to learn from experience. Regardless of age, education, or occupation, if we are spiritually alive, we will be teachable; that is, we will be able to be stirred, enlightened, and changed by life's experiences.

Three Pillars of Learning

Historian Benjamin Barber has said: "I don't divide the world into the weak and the strong, or the successes and the failures, those who make it or those who don't. I divide the world into learners and nonlearners." What distinguishes learners from nonlearners? Perhaps English writer Benjamin Disraeli gave us a clue when he identified these as the three "pillars" of learning: "seeing much, studying much, and suffering much." Let's take a brief look at each one.

Seeing much. All learning begins with seeing; that is, it begins with noticing things, with paying attention to what is happening around us. Good teachers know this. They realize, for example, that the success of any lesson largely depends on getting and sustaining their students' attention. Good teaching is nothing less than helping students see more.

Studying much. To be a learner, however, it is not enough simply to see much. As Disraeli said, we must also study much. This means we must reflect on what we see. Horticulturalist Rebecca Rupp defined science as "a long and careful look beneath and beyond the world's skin." We can say that all learning involves a long and careful look beneath and beyond the surface of things. This kind of reflecting can prove beneficial, for, as someone has wisely said, "It is not experience, but *thinking* about experience, that gives wisdom."

Suffering Much. The third pillar of learning is suffering. If we want to learn, we must open ourselves to the possibility of pain.

Even as I write these words, I cringe, for I wish there was another way to learn—a painless way. Although learning sometimes can be a pleasure and a joy, more often than not the greatest lessons we learn in life entail some form of suffering. When the little girl was asked how she learned to skate, for example, she replied, "By getting up every time I fell." On the road to knowledge and wisdom, we are apt to fall many times.

Mistakes and Failure

If we have a healthy spirituality we will have a healthy attitude toward all the falls we take in life, toward all the mistakes we make. We will agree with Richard Rohr, a Franciscan who lectures on spirituality, who said, "The mistakes we make are the best teachers in the world." We will likewise subscribe to the adage, "Those who make mistakes make everything else as well!" We will see our mistakes not as roadblocks to moral perfection, but as stepping-stones to greater humility and compassion. As English nun Janet Stuart wrote almost a hundred years ago: "We all blunder and trip and crawl and tumble and pick ourselves up again. But we are going on, and please God, each mistake we make leaves us a little humbler and so nearer to God."

Similarly, if our spirituality is healthy, we will not be devastated when we experience failure. We will recall how we fell down many times before we learned to walk and how we sank the first time we tried to swim. We will remember that Babe Ruth, on his way to hitting 714 home runs, struck out 1,330 times. And Dr. Seuss' first book was rejected by twenty-three editors before the twenty-fourth one bought it. Most coaches, no matter how good they are, must learn to deal with failure. It is no surprise then, when asked what his favorite saying was, football coach Don Shula replied, "Success is not forever; failure is not fatal."

Teachability and the Gospels

What do the gospels teach us about teachability? First, they tell us that Jesus himself was teachable. Even as a young boy, Jesus is shown sitting with the elders in the temple, listening to them and asking them questions. Jesus subscribed to the three "pillars of learning" too. He was good at seeing much and studying much. He had the habit of looking beneath surfaces and beyond appearances. He gazed at a gruff and stubborn fisherman named Simon, for example, and saw a dynamic and devoted leader. He watched a poor widow drop two tiny coins into the temple treasury and pronounced her the most generous giver of all.

Jesus was always urging his disciples to "study" life and thus to learn from it. Over and over again he exhorts his followers with words such as these: look, listen, take care, remember, watch, and pray—words that induce learning. He frequently asked his followers questions, thus encouraging them to reflect further on issues at hand. He asked: "What did you go out to the wilderness to look at?" (Mt 11:7); "Whose head is this, and whose title?" (Mk 12:16); "And the seven [loaves] for the four thousand, how many baskets full of broken pieces did you collect?" (Mk 8:20); "But who do you say that I am?" (Lk 9:20)

Perhaps Jesus shows his teachability the most, however, through his willingness to suffer. From the very beginning of his life, Jesus was utterly vulnerable. He was born of a young couple in a poor country totally dominated by a foreign military power. As a child, he was forced with his parents to become a refugee in a foreign land. Later, when Jesus begins his public ministry, he opens himself up to even more pain. He chooses for his apostles twelve very ordinary and very human men. One eventually betrays him into the hands of his enemies, while the remaining eleven desert him in his hour of need. During his passion, Jesus experiences first hand the agony of defeat. In fact, from the perspective of Good Friday, Jesus was a total failure. For there he was, after only a brief period of success, being executed on a cross, a common criminal hanging between two run-of-the-mill thieves.

From the perspective of Easter, however, Jesus is not a failure at all; he is success personified. It was precisely through his embrace of suffering and death that Jesus achieved his ultimate triumph: rebirth into new and everlasting life. What's more, as Christians we believe Jesus has the power to take us with him into his kingdom of eternal life.

In her book *Seek Treasures in Small Fields*, Joan Puls writes, "We have the potential for rebirth and transformation, as long as we remain vulnerable to new experiences, to all that we have not yet learned." She implies, I think, that all learning results in some form of transformation, some degree of conversion. That is precisely why teachability is so essential for the spiritual life, for, in the final analysis, the spiritual life is all about conversion. Every Ash Wednesday we hear these words, "Reform your lives and believe in the gospel." Teachability makes such reform possible. Teachability is the prerequisite for conversion.

I began this chapter with samples from the book *Live and Learn and Pass It On*. I would like to conclude by sharing with you three things I have learned in life:

• I have learned that no cupcake ever tastes as good as it looks.

• I have learned that teachability is essential for spiritual growth.

• And I have learned that I still have many more things to learn.

Questions for Reflection

1. To what extent do you agree with the three quotations at the beginning of this chapter?

2. What do you think of the three pillars of learning: seeing much, studying much, suffering much? Can you think of any other pillars?

3. How do you feel when you make a mistake? Why do you feel this way?

4. Have you ever experienced failure? How did you deal with it?

Practice

I will draw up a list of at least ten things I have learned in life and share my list with God in prayer.

Make Me More Teachable

Loving God,
        make me more teachable.
Help me to pay closer attention

to the world around and inside of me.
Help me to look beneath surfaces
and beyond appearances.
Lead me to reflect on my experiences.
May I heed Jesus' words every day:
look, listen, take care,
remember, watch, pray.
Coax me to be more open to life
despite the possibility of pain,
knowing that life's greatest lessons
often entail some form of suffering.
And finally, God,
give me a positive attitude
toward all the mistakes I make.
Help me to see them
not as roadblocks to perfection
but as stepping-stones
to greater humility and compassion.
Every time I trip or stumble,
tumble or fall,
may I pick myself up (with your help)
and continue on my journey toward you.
Amen.

Tolerance

Keeping Our Parachutes Open

I begin to suspect that a man's bewilderment is the measure of his wisdom. —Nathaniel Hawthorne

I would define fundamentalism as a defense against the overtones of life, the richness and polytheism of imagination.
—Thomas Moore

Heaven will display far more variety than Hell. —C.S. Lewis

There is a joke about a paratroop instructor who was teaching his class the basics of parachuting. He carefully explained to his students how to open their parachutes, adding that each of them would also be wearing a second parachute just in case the first one didn't open. One student asked, "Sir, what happens if the second chute doesn't open either?" The instructor replied, "That, young man, is what we call 'jumping to a conclusion.'"

Another sign of a healthy spirituality is tolerance, that is, the ability not to jump to conclusions. This means we are slow to judge people and situations. Rather, we are able to live graciously with loose ends, ambiguity, and diversity in our lives. Following the advice of the poet Rilke, we are able to be "patient toward all that is unsolved in (our) heart." We subscribe to the maxim: "Minds are like parachutes: they work only when open."

Ambiguity

I have a friend who maintains that eighty-five percent of life is ambiguous; that is, eighty-five percent is neither clearly good nor clearly evil. Although some might disagree with his estimate, most would agree that *much* in life is ambiguous. People, for example, are seldom totally good or totally evil. Actions are seldom completely right or completely wrong. When faced with ambiguity, many of us find it hard to be open-minded. We would prefer a world divided into neat compartments labeled good and evil, right and wrong, black and white. We crave certainty: Is this situation good or bad? Is this new movement beneficial or harmful? Is this desire coming from God or the devil?

Jesus appreciated the ambiguities of life. On more than one occasion, he urged his disciples to keep an open mind and not to jump to conclusions. In the parable of the barren fig tree, for example, Jesus told about the owner of a fig tree who ordered his gardener to cut the tree down. After all, it hadn't produced a fig in three years. The gardener, however, pleaded with the owner saying, "Sir, let it alone for one more year, until I dig around it and put manure on it. If it bears fruit next year, well and good; but if not, you can cut it down" (Lk 13:8–9). Through this parable, Jesus was saying, "Don't judge too hastily. Don't give up too soon. With a little more care, even the barren might bear fruit."

The parable of the weeds among the wheat offers a similar message. The owner of a large farm sowed wheat in his fields. While he was asleep, an enemy came in and sowed weeds among the wheat. Later, when the wheat came up, so did the weeds. The servants wanted to rush into the fields and pull all the weeds out. But the owner cautioned them against doing this, saying, "No; for in gathering the weeds you would uproot the wheat along with them. Let both of them grow together until harvest" (Mt 13:29–30). In this parable Jesus was saying, "Don't rush in. Be patient—lest you inadvertently destroy the good with the bad."

Ambiguity is a reality of daily life. A healthy spirituality, knowing this, fosters open-mindedness and patience. It reminds us that certainty is not necessarily a goal in life. As Anthony De Mello, SJ, warns us in *Wellsprings*, "Certainty is the sin of bigots, terrorists, and Pharisees." Uncertainty, however, can be disconcerting. The rise of religious fundamentalism in our own day is probably a reaction to the discomfort of ambiguity. As author Robertson Davies has said, "Fanaticism is...overcompensation for doubt."

The Gift of Diversity

How do we know how open-minded and patient we are? One indication is how tolerant we are of diversity. Do we see diversity as blessing or curse, gift or bane? There is little doubt what scripture thinks of diversity. It clearly presents diversity as a good thing. In Genesis, for example, we find that diversity is the fundamental characteristic of God's creation. God is shown creating a wide variety of things: light and darkness, sun and moon, oceans and dry land, birds and fish, man and woman. And God pronounces this diversity "good." We could ask ourselves: how well do we recognize and appreciate diversity?

Recently I had a vivid experience of the diversity in nature when my father gave me some flower and seed catalogues to look at. One night before crawling into bed, I picked up a forty-page catalog devoted exclusively to tulips. As I slowly leafed through its pages, I was utterly amazed at the variety of tulips I saw. Pictured were red, yellow, and white ones—colors I was familiar with. But then I saw dozens of other colors including light and dark blues, deep purple, bright and pale pinks, orange, and even chartreuse. Some tulips were one color, but others were striped or splashed with several different colors. Some tulips were quite small, while others had blooms over ten inches wide. The catalog gave me a greater appreciation of the incredible diversity in the world of tulips. I remember thinking: if there is so much diversity in this one kind of flower, then how much more diversity is there among all the other species in nature—including Homo sapiens!

Celebrating Diversity in People

There is great diversity among human beings. Physically we differ from each other in things such as size, body structure, skin color, and facial features. We also differ from one another mentally, emotionally, psychologically, and spiritually. One of the greatest challenges of a healthy spirituality is learning to tolerate the differences we find in one another and not to view these differences as threats to ourselves. Moreover, a healthy spirituality should lead us to celebrate our differences and to see them as a reflection of God's beneficence and creativity.

St. Paul celebrated diversity. In his letter to the Corinthians, he says: "Now there are varieties of gifts, but the same Spirit; and there are varieties of services, but the same Lord; and there are varieties of activities, but it is the same God who activates all of them in everyone" (1 Cor 12:4–6).

Jesus, too, appreciated and celebrated diversity in people. In the gospels we see him choosing a diverse group of men to be his apostles. Several were fisherman, one was a tax collector, one a religious zealot. A few were outspoken, while others were reticent. Some were probably older than he, while at least one, John, was considerably younger. And Jesus did not limit discipleship to men only. No, he invited women to be his followers as well, even choosing them to be the first recipients of the good news of his resurrection. Jesus looked beyond the differences of personality, occupation, age, and gender and saw the oneness of humanity.

Jesus was also respectful of the uniqueness of individuals. He agreed to meet Nicodemus under the cover of darkness, for example, because he was sensitive to Nicodemus' hesitancy to be seen with him. Jesus allowed the sinful woman to anoint him extravagantly with perfume, because he sensed that this was the way she knew best to show affection. Jesus' pedagogy also reveals his appreciation of the diversity of his listeners. He tailored his lessons to reach a wide range of individuals. To farmers he spoke in images of fields and wheat, to housewives in images of bread making and housecleaning, to builders in images of stone and mortar.

But it is in his teachings on love that Jesus addressed the challenge of diversity most directly. We are to love our neighbor, he said. In one way, such a command might not be too difficult. After all, our neighbors are often people like ourselves. They basically look like us, dress like us, talk like us, and act like us. It is relatively easy to like people similar to ourselves. But then Jesus gives us another command: we are to love our enemy. What a challenge this is for us, for it asks us to love even those individuals we perceive as totally different, as "other," as "them." Jesus' command to love our enemies is nothing more than a call to tolerate maximum diversity. It is a command to give others—even those who oppose us—the benefit of the doubt.

Once, when I was teaching high school, a student came to me to complain about another student. I listened to her attentively as she enumerated everything that was wrong with this other individual. I let her know I understood what she was saying, but then I began asking her some questions in an attempt to lead her to be less judgmental and more tolerant of the other person. Immediately she became annoyed with me and blurted out, "You know what's wrong with you? You always give people the benefit of the doubt!" She meant her words as a criticism I suspect, but I took them as a compliment.

In conclusion, we can say that ambiguity takes many forms in our lives: doubt, uncertainty, confusion, bewilderment, controversy. Diversity, too, takes many forms and often can be just as unsettling as ambiguity. But Jesus, through both word and example, urges us to approach ambiguity and diversity with patience, trust, and tolerance. In short, Jesus reminds us to keep our parachutes open.

Questions for Reflection

1. To what extent do you agree or disagree with the quotations at the beginning of this chapter?

2. Name some of the ambiguities you have experienced or are experiencing in your life. What helps you to deal with these ambiguities patiently and with an open mind?

3. Name some of the diversities in people that you appreciate or enjoy.

4. Has anyone ever given you the benefit of the doubt? If so, how did that make you feel?

Practice

I will give someone the benefit of the doubt today.

Help Me to Keep an Open Mind

Loving God,
  help me to keep an open mind.
Help me to live graciously with ambiguity
  and to be more patient toward all
  that is unsolved in my heart.
Let me hear you say to me each day,
  "Don't judge too hastily;
  don't give up too soon.
With time and care
  even this barren thing may bear fruit."
Or: "Don't rush into that field
  to kill all those weeds,
  lest you destroy my precious wheat
  nestling beside them."
Patient God,
  help me to tolerate
  and celebrate diversity
  in all the many forms
  I encounter it—
  especially in people.
Help me, like you,
  to pronounce diversity "good."
May I, like Jesus, see diversity
  as a faint reflection
  of your beneficence and creativity.
Amen.

J<u>O</u>Y

Does Your God Know How to Dance?

A gloomy Christian is a contradiction in terms.
—William Barclay

Laughter is a form of internal jogging. —Norman Cousins

He who has the courage to laugh is almost as much a master of the world as he who is ready to die. —Giacomo Leopardi

---

The late columnist Erma Bombeck talked of being in church one Sunday and seeing a little boy who was turning around and smiling at everyone. He wasn't doing anything more than that. Just smiling. Suddenly his mother yanked him around and yelled at him in a whisper loud enough for everyone to hear: "Stop that grinning! You're in church!"

This true story illustrates how some people view the Christian faith. They see faith as a serious business. Only a serious business. For such people, smiling has no place in church and no place in their spirituality. Such a view is mistaken, of course, for one of the hallmarks of our Christian faith is joy. John Henry Newman said that "the chief grace of primitive Christianity (was) joy." We could add that another trait of a healthy spirituality is joy and laughter.

We might wonder, then, why don't we smile more in church? Why is there a strain of gloom in Christianity? Why, for example, do the pictures of Jesus almost never show him smiling? After all, Jesus was someone who knew how to have a good time. He worked his first miracle at a wedding reception. He frequently dined in people's homes. Jesus was incredibly approachable. People of both genders and all ages flocked to him—including little children. And, as we know, most kids (as well as adults) are naturally drawn to happy, upbeat individuals. Joy was a major theme of Jesus' parables, while his principal image for the kingdom of God was a festive party.

Some individuals think Christianity tends to be serious because Jesus died such a horrible death on the cross. But contrary to what the faces of some Christians project, the heart of the Christian message is not the cross, it is the empty tomb. It is not suffering and death, it is resurrection and life. Shouldn't this message make us joyful people?

Others argue that Christianity took a turn toward "doom and gloom" with the early Christian persecutions. If you are standing in the coliseum about to be eaten by lions, it is pretty difficult, I imagine, to come up with a good one-liner. Yet, the eyewitness accounts of those early martyrdoms tell us that many of those Christians went to their deaths singing. Our conclusion can only be this: those martyrs must have seen something beyond the lions and death. And that, of course, is precisely true. In most cases, joy and laughter are possible only when we see something beyond the immediate circumstances of life. In other words, there is a definite link between joy and humor and the vision of faith.

Faith and Humor

An older man won millions of dollars in the state lottery. Since he had a weak heart, his wife enlisted the pastor's help to gently break the good news to her husband. The priest did a fine job. The winner was so happy, he exclaimed, "Father, I want to give half of my winnings to the parish." And with that, the pastor dropped dead.

Why do we laugh at such a story? The Canadian writer Stephen Leacock defined humor as "the kindly contemplation of the incongruities of life." The word "kindly" is important here, for there is a kind of humor that is "unkindly." This is the humor that delights in another's misfortune or pain. The villain in the old silent movies, for example, displayed this type of humor when he laughed as he tied poor Nell to the railroad tracks. Sarcasm and mockery are also strains of unkindly humor. The humor we're talking about in this chapter is only the kindly kind.

Leacock's definition of humor mentions "the incongruities of life." In the story above, we laugh at the incongruities involved: the wife is concerned that the good news will cause her husband to have a heart attack. But he doesn't. Yet when the man tells the pastor he's going to donate half of the money to the parish, the pastor has the heart attack. That anyone could be that generous to a parish is the *real* shock!

True humor sees the incongruities of life against the backdrop of the mighty congruities of life, such as God's unfailing love for us, our fallen but redeemed nature, the ultimate triumph of good. The person who has no faith in such congruities sees only part of reality. Those early Christian martyrs could sing as they were being eaten by lions because they saw beyond their death to God's unfailing love for them. Death was not the end for them, but the birth into new life. Cal Samra says this in his book *The Joyful Jesus,* "There is an old saying that 'he who laughs last, laughs best.' And who had the largest and most robust laugh in history? The resurrected Jesus, who rose from the dead and laughed all the devils away."

Growing in Joy and Laughter

If joy and laughter are traits of a healthy spirituality, then how can we keep these qualities alive in our lives? There are many ways we can do this, no doubt, but I would like to suggest four.

John Powell, SJ, once said, "If you're happy, let your face know." Maybe we could begin to be more joyful by taking a peek in the mirror and asking ourselves: does my face look like the face of someone who has heard the good news of the gospel? Does my face show that I really believe God loves us, that Jesus is my friend, that there is life after death?

A second way to grow in joy is to ask ourselves: what is my image of God? Is God a stern taskmaster lurking in the dark, ready to pounce on me? Or is God more like the father in the parable of the prodigal son, running toward me with open arms, ready to hug me? German philosopher Friedrich Nietzsche said, "I should only believe in a God who would know how to dance." Does our God know how to dance? (With a Czech name like Svoboda, I know my God knows how to polka!)

Thirdly, we can grow in joy by examining our attitude toward both sorrow and joy. G.K. Chesterton wrote that, for Christians, sorrow is "the superficial," whereas joy is "the fundamental thing." Sorrow is only an "innocent interlude," but joy is "the permanent pulsation of the soul." This is not to minimize the pains and sorrow we experience in life. But can we still trust in the love of God even in our tears?

A fourth way we can grow is by periodically taking stock of our sense of humor. The devil, they say, can't stand the sound of laughter. How often do we laugh? How often do we cause others to laugh? I confess, when I pick up a copy of *Reader's Digest* or *Catholic Digest,* the first thing I read are all the jokes and humorous stories. I also religiously read the comics every day in the newspaper and frequently cut out cartoons to send to friends. In a world where we are bombarded every day with bad news from all over the globe, we Christians of today have to work harder, I think, to hang on to joy and our sense of humor.

Time Out for a Few Jokes

There's no better way to conclude a chapter on joy and laughter than by sharing some humorous stories. Here are a few which happen to have a religious slant.

The teacher was preparing her class for their first confession. She asked, "What's the first thing we have to do before we are forgiven?" One little boy answered, "We have to commit some sins."

The parish priest said to his congregation: "I have bad news, good news, and bad news for you. The bad news is that the church needs a new roof. The good news is, we have the money. The bad news for you? The money is in your pockets."

Some people claim they don't go to church because of the hypocrisy they see there. But A.R. Adams tells them, "Don't stay away from Church because there are so many hypocrites. There's always room for one more!"

During the Christmas play the children were allowed to ad lib.

When St. Joseph asked the innkeeper if he had any room, the innkeeper replied, "Are you kidding? We're booked clear through Easter!"

And finally, one of my favorite prayers is this short one by St. Teresa of Avila: "From silly devotions and from sour-faced saints, good Lord, deliver us."

Questions for Reflection

1. Do any of the quotations at the beginning of this chapter resonate with you today?

2. Do you agree that there is a connection between faith and a sense of humor? Why or why not?

3. Was there anything in this chapter that resonated with your own experience? If so, what?

4. What brings you joy in life? What helps you to keep your sense of humor?

Practice

I will do something today that brings others and myself joy and laughter.

I Ask for Joy and Laughter

Dear God,
    I ask for joy and laughter
    to see with the vision of faith,
    to view the incongruities of life
    against the backdrop
    of your unconditional love.
May my face be the face of someone
    who has heard the good news.
When sorrow and pain enter my life,
    help me to see them not as finalities
    but as mere interludes,
    and joy and laughter
    as the ultimate realities of life.
God, make me more like Jesus,

your joy-filled son.
Help me to trust in your love,
    even in my tears.
For I truly believe:
    good will triumph over evil,
    Jesus has the last laugh,
    and you, dear God,
    know how to dance!
Amen.

Interdependence

Orange Frogs and Yellow Canaries

Nothing in the world is single,
All things by a law divine
In each other's being mingle.   —Percy Bysshe Shelley

A person wrapped up in himself is a very small package.
                              —Anonymous

...thou canst not stir a flower
Without troubling a star.   —Francis Thompson

Not long ago I was watching a nature program on TV concerning a rare species of orange frogs living somewhere in a remote jungle. The narrator said scientists noticed the frogs were suddenly and mysteriously dying in large numbers. The scientists were concerned, for they feared that the sudden death of the frogs was due to some significant yet undetected change in the earth's atmosphere—a change that, in time, could prove just as fatal to human beings.

This TV program reminded me of another story I was told as a child. Years ago when miners went down into the coal mines, they used to take a small bird in a cage with them. (For some reason, I always pictured a yellow canary.) If any poisonous gases began seeping into the mine shaft while the miners worked, the bird would be affected first. Therefore, if the bird suddenly got sick or (worse yet) keeled over, the miners would immediately evacuate the mine. (I only hope they took the canary with them!)

Orange frogs and yellow canaries. Both stories attest to this great truth: all creation is interconnected. To paraphrase the old African-American spiritual, frogs are connected to people, rocks to stars, hummingbirds to redwood trees, oceans to geraniums. As writer Annie Dillard said, "All life is an interconnected membrane, a weft of linkages like chain mail." If we have a healthy spirituality we are mindful of this basic interconnectedness of all things, this interdependence of everything.

New Sin, New Virtue

In a recent article, journalist Monica Furlong wrote, "I feel we are in the process of charting a new sin. The new sin is the inability, or the refusal, to look at the implications of everything we do in a very much wider context than in the past." In other words, the new sin is our refusal to be mindful of interdependence. It is our failure to acknowledge that what we do in New York City has repercussions in New Delhi, Kiev, and Tahiti—and vice versa. And what we do today has consequences for tomorrow. We see the devastating effects of this new sin in the pollution of our lakes and rivers, in the violence bred by excessive nationalism, and in the obscenely unfair distribution of the world's wealth. On a more personal level, we see evidence of this sin every time we make a decision without considering its ramifications for people and things beyond ourselves. Or when we audaciously assume that our limited point of view is the *only* and *correct* point of view.

With every new sin comes the need for a new virtue. According to Furlong the new virtue for our day is this: "the determination to connect." It is the virtue of "loving the earth with all its wonders and doing our best to heal its creatures."

How do we practice this new virtue? How do we grow in the determination to connect? I suggest three ways: by listening, by living in community, and by growing in compassion. These three ways are, of course, interconnected!

Listening

The Stoic philosopher Epictetus said that God gave us two ears and one mouth, so that we would listen twice as much as we speak. One way we grow in our determination to connect is by listening. This means we take time to listen to the world around us—even to orange frogs. It means we listen to other people too. The well-known psychiatrist Karl Menninger believed that the experience of not being listened to actually made people unwell. Conversely, the experience of being listened to made them well again.

Theologian Dietrich Bonhoeffer also spoke of the importance of listening. He lamented the fact that Christians talked too much and listened too little, adding that one who no longer listened to his brother or sister soon would no longer be listening to God. Such a person, said Bonhoeffer, would eventually "be doing nothing but prattling in the presence of God." And such prattling "is the beginning of the death of the spiritual life."

So, we grow in connectedness by listening to creation, to other people, and to God. In addition, we grow by listening to our own thoughts and feelings. This means we take time to ask ourselves questions such as these: What do I really want and desire from life? How am I feeling about this particular situation? What effect will my decision have on others and for tomorrow?

Living in Community

If we truly listen to the world around us and to our own thoughts and feelings, we cannot help but grow in the awareness of our oneness with each other, in the realization that we are living in a community. This appreciation of community is perhaps more important for us today than ever before, for we live in a culture that deifies autonomy and self-sufficiency, in a world that downplays concern for the so-called common good. "Have it your way!" "Look out for number one!" "Me first!" are just a few of the popular slogans that reflect our culture's excessive individualism.

In his book *The Good Society*, Robert Bellah notes that a symbol of our society's lack of community is the microwave oven—a convenience that has made it possible, unfortunately, to do away with the concept of a shared meal. Instead of a family coming together to prepare, eat, and clean up after Sunday dinner, for example, each member all too often "zaps" his or her own favorite prepared dish, eats it alone and in haste, and dashes off to the next activity. We see this loss of a sense of community expressed in other ways too: in the obsessive pursuit of private agendas, in the widespread feeling of isolation, and in the escalation of consumerism as a desperate attempt to assuage loneliness.

Individuals with a healthy spirituality live the belief that we are profoundly interconnected to God, others, and all creation. Consequently, they willingly contribute to the common good—even in small ways like recycling trash, donating to a scholarship fund, or volunteering in a soup kitchen. They realize that this belief in community is not an option. It is, as our poets, ecologists, theologians, and sociologists keep telling us, essential for the survival of our planet.

Growing in Compassion

Listening to others and regaining our sense of community will lead to compassion. The dictionary tells us that compassion is the sympathetic awareness of another's distress coupled with the desire to do something to alleviate it. In other words, it is the ability to slip into another's shoes—whether they be moccasins, sandals, sneakers, clogs, or even bare feet—and to experience what the other person is suffering. So crucial is compassion to humanity that Dostoevsky dubbed it "the chief law of human existence."

Compassion is crucial, yes, but it is not always easy. In his book *Strangers*, Dean Koontz remarks, "We care. It is our curse." Writer Eugene Kennedy agrees that compassion is difficult. He writes, "It is easier to reject a hurting world than it is to embrace it with compassion."

Scripture speaks often of the importance and challenge of compassion. There is no better example of this than Jesus' parable of the Good Samaritan (Lk 10:25–37). One day a lawyer asks Jesus, "Who is my neighbor?" Jesus responds with a story. He says that a certain man, a Jew, was on his way down from Jerusalem to Jericho when he fell victim to a gang of robbers who stripped him, beat him, and left him half dead on the side of the road. A priest happens by and, seeing the man lying there, decides not to stop. No reason is given, but perhaps the priest assumes the man is already dead. To touch a corpse would make the priest unclean for worship. Not willing to chance that, the priest continues on his way.

Next a Levite passes by and does the same thing. Finally a Samaritan happens by. Samaritans, remember, were the enemies of the Jews. This man sees the battered man and is "moved with compassion at the sight" (Lk 10:33). In other words, the Samaritan realizes his connectedness with this man. He knows how he would feel if he were wearing this man's sandals. So he pours oil on the man's wounds, bandages them, lifts the man onto his own animal, and takes him to an inn. After nursing him through the night, the Samaritan pays the innkeeper to care for the man, promising to pay him more if necessary upon his return.

After telling the parable, Jesus asks the lawyer, "Which of these three, in your opinion, was neighbor to the robbers' victim?" The lawyer answers, "The one who treated him with mercy." To which Jesus replies, "Go and do likewise."

The lawyer had asked Jesus, "Who is my neighbor?" He was looking for a clear, simple legal definition. Instead, Jesus answers his question with a stunning story of the incredible compassion one man showed to his enemy. Jesus' parable removes the discussion from the realm of philosophical speculation to the plane of real life. His "Go and do likewise" is another way of saying to the lawyer (and to us!), "Let your sense of connectedness lead you to perform similar acts of love."

If our spirituality is healthy, it will enable us to uncover, as Joan Puls says in *Every Bush Is Burning*, the "very real and very visible interconnectedness that makes all of creation one." It will then help us find "our own place in the 'flow' of life, entering the mystery and becoming part of the universal 'dance.'"

Questions for Reflection

1. How do you respond to each of the three quotations at the beginning of this chapter?

2. Reflect on a time when you experienced your connectedness

with creation and/or with other people. What factors contributed to this experience? What effect did the experience have on you?

3. Are you a good listener? If so, what helps you to be one? If not, what can you do to become a better listener?

4. Think of a time when someone showed you compassion. What effect did his or her compassion have on you?

Practice

I will love my neighbor today; that is, I will concretely show compassion to someone in need today.

Help Me to See Connections

Good and gracious God,
  help me to see connections
  between frogs and people,
  flowers and stars,
  oceans and redwood trees.
May I look at the implications
  of everything I do
  in a much wider context than before,
  and always consider the impact
  today's decisions
  will have on tomorrow.
Help me to listen better
  to creation, to others,
  to my own thoughts and feelings,
  and most of all to you.
Give me a deeper appreciation
  for the unique contribution I can make
  to the common good.
And finally, God,
  may I grow in compassion,
  by being ready and willing
  to slip into another's shoes,
  and so find my own place
  in the universal dance of life.
Amen.

Perseverance

Can You Wait
to Eat the Marshmallows?

He conquers who endures.   —Italian proverb

Genius is protracted patience.   —French proverb

*Perseverance is the hard work you do after you get tired of doing
the hard work you already did.*   —Newt Gingrich

An eighty-seven-year-old nun lived in her community's large
health care center. To put it kindly, she was not known for her
cheerful disposition. Yet everyday she would shuffle down the
hall with her cane to pray aloud to the statue of St. Thérèse the
Little Flower—a saint who died at the age of twenty-four. One day
another sister overheard the elderly nun saying to the statue: "If
you had lived as long as I have, you wouldn't be a saint either!"

The true story makes a good point: perseverance in virtue is no
easy task. Whereas it might be easy to be virtuous for a short period of time (the week before Santa Claus comes, for example), it is
not easy to be good for a long period of time (for the other fifty-
one weeks of the year—let alone for eighty-seven years!).
Perseverance is never easy. That's one reason we admire perseverance so much in whatever form we see it. We admire athletes, for
example, who train rigorously for many years just for the chance

to compete in the Olympics. We admire St. Monica who prayed for the conversion of her son, Augustine, for over thirty years! And we admire couples like my parents who have been married to each other for over fifty-eight years!

Perseverance, when it is a virtue, is a trait of a healthy spirituality. By saying "when it is a virtue," I am implying that it may not always be one. Sometimes perseverance may be mere stubbornness. The question is then: when is perseverance a virtue and when is it not?

From Acorn to Oak Tree

To answer that question, let us begin by defining perseverance. It is the ability to persist in an undertaking over a long period of time despite counterinfluences, periodic setbacks, or bouts of discouragement. Synonyms for perseverance include endurance, steadfastness, constancy, and stability. But it would be wrong to equate perseverance with merely staying in one place or sticking to one thing. We all know people who stayed in marriages that were hopelessly dead, or people who stayed in relationships that were totally destructive. Similarly, we know individuals who stayed in unfulfilling jobs, even when they were offered something better, simply because they lacked the courage to change. These individuals have perseverance, yes, but not necessarily the kind we can admire or call virtuous.

When, then, is perseverance a virtue? We can answer that question by asking another one: what does God call us to persevere in? Jesus gives us the answer: love. God calls us to love God and love our neighbor. No more, no less. Perseverance is a virtue if it enables us to do this. If it does not, it may be mere tenacity. At judgment time, God will not ask us how long we persevered in a certain vocation or place or relationship or occupation. God will ask us how well we persevered in loving.

I like the adage that says, "Persevere! Remember that the greatest oak tree was once a little nut that held its ground!" In one sense, every oak tree is an acorn that persevered. But the acorn did not persevere in remaining an acorn. It persevered in becoming an oak. Over time the little nut was gradually and radically transformed. Using this metaphor, we can say that God calls us not to be stubborn acorns, but to become majestic oak trees. And that takes perseverance.

Discipline and Vision

What factors enable us to persevere in this lifelong undertaking of radical transformation? Although there are many, I would like to focus on two: 1) self-discipline, and 2) a vision of the future. They are interrelated.

My favorite definition of discipline is the one by author David Campbell: "Discipline is remembering what you want." Discipline always involves self-control, but not self-control for its own sake. Rather, it is self-control for the sake of something we want in the future. Therefore, the clearer our vision is of what we want in the future, the better our chances are of mustering up and sustaining the self-discipline needed to achieve that vision. In other words, the sharper the vision, the more likely the perseverance. I have a middle-aged friend, for example, who, when she went on a diet, put a picture of her younger, thinner self on the refrigerator door. The picture was a visual reminder to her of what she wanted to look like in the future. She knew her vision could become a reality if she had enough self-discipline to stay out of the refrigerator and stay on her diet.

Educators know how important it is to keep the vision of the future before the eyes of their students. That's why so many schools sponsor alumni career days where they invite successful former students to come back and talk to the current students. The alumni, through their very presence, offer the students a vision of themselves in the future, a vision that can encourage them to stay in school and persevere in achieving their goals.

In order to persevere, however, we must have more than a clear vision of what we want. We must *really* want it. A few years back I taught with a young man who had been an excellent baseball player in high school and college. Upon graduating, he played for a couple of years in the Yankees farm system. Eventually he made the decision to quit. He told me, "I found out I didn't want to be a major league baseball player bad enough." We will persevere in trying to achieve our vision only if we want it bad enough. (I, for one, was glad my colleague forsook a career in baseball, for he is now directly influencing many kids as a fine teacher and coach!)

Can You Wait to Eat the Marshmallows?

For years psychologists have been asking the question: which personality traits most determine success in life? Which traits enable people to persevere in achieving their goals? Recently a study claimed to come up with one answer: impulse control which is "the ability to delay impulse in the service of a goal." One part of the study, conducted over a twelve-year period, used marshmallows to test four-year-old children.

The test is a simple one. A psychologist sits at a desk with a four-year-old and puts two marshmallows in front of the child. The psychologist then tells the child that she is going out of the room for twenty minutes to run an errand. The child is free to eat the two marshmallows while she's gone, she says, but if the child waits until the psychologist comes back, he or she can have four marshmallows. The psychologist makes it very clear to the child: two marshmallows now or four marshmallows later. Then she leaves the room. Meanwhile a hidden camera records the child's behavior.

Some children grabbed the marshmallows immediately and ate them. But others were able to wait despite an obvious struggle. To prevent themselves from eating the marshmallows, for example, some children covered their eyes, talked or sang to themselves, turned their backs on the marshmallows, or even tried to sleep. The study claims that four-year-olds who do not eat the marshmallows have a better chance of persevering in achieving their goals in life, for they have grasped the concept of delayed gratification.

Perseverance and Scripture

Scripture is replete with references to perseverance. On many occasions Jesus encouraged his disciples to persevere. In explaining his parable of the sower, for example, Jesus said that the seed that fell on rich soil represented those who, upon hearing the word of God, "hold it fast in an honest and good heart, and bear fruit with patient endurance" (Lk 8:15). When warning his disciples of the persecutions to come, Jesus promised them that "the one who endures to the end will be saved" (Mt 10:22).

Throughout scripture we find exhortations to perseverance even when the actual word is not used. Barnabas and Paul urged the early Christian community to "continue in the grace of God" (Acts 13:43); Paul encouraged the Corinthians to be firm and "steadfast" (1 Cor 15:58); and the author of the letter of Peter told his listeners to "beware that you are not carried away...and lose your own stability" (2 Pt 3:17). Be faithful, be steadfast, be stable. In other words, persevere.

In other places scripture tells us that perseverance will be rewarded. St. Paul told the Romans that they would be blessed with "eternal life" by "patiently doing good" (Rom 2:7). Similarly, St. James wrote that those who "persevere...will be blessed in their doing" (Jas 1:25).

Jesus himself gives us a beautiful example of perseverance and steadfastness. It is good for us to ask ourselves, how was Jesus able to persevere to the end? What enabled him to endure his particular trials and temptations? The answer is simple. Jesus persevered the same way we persevere: by remembering he was loved by God. (But that's a whole other chapter!)

For now we can conclude this chapter by recalling what Genesis tells us: that we are made in the image and likeness of God. Throughout scripture we are told that one of God's outstanding attributes is perseverance. In both the Hebrew Scriptures and the New Testament, God is depicted as someone who never gives up. God is the Eternally Patient One, the Almighty Steadfast One, the Infinitely Faithful One. Or (if you prefer) God is the one with indefatigable stamina, unyielding determination, inexhaustible pluck. Like the persistent widow in Jesus' parable, God is forever seeking us, calling us, pursuing us, bothering us—all in an effort to convince us we are loved by God and we must love our brothers and sisters as God loves them.

In short, our God is the God of Perseverance. That fact is our hope for salvation.

Questions for Reflection

1. Do you agree or disagree with the three quotations at the beginning of this chapter?

2. Think of someone you know who has demonstrated perseverance. What were some of the obstacles he or she faced? What factors do you think enabled this individual to persevere?

3. To what extent do you have self-discipline? How have you shown that you are able to live with delayed gratification?

4. Are there any sentences in this chapter that you really resonate with? that you question or take exception to?

Practice

I will reflect on one aspect of my vision for the future and discuss with God in prayer what concrete steps I can take to realize that vision.

You Are the God of Perseverance

Dear God,
  you are the God of perseverance.
And I am made in your image and likeness.
Help me to persevere
  in the one thing necessary: loving.
Give me a positive view of discipline,
  one that sees it
  as remembering what I really want.
Show me how important
  my vision for the future is
  and lead me to want that vision bad enough,
  that I willingly make the sacrifices needed
  to bring it into being.
Give me the strength
  to forgo current, fleeting pleasures
  if they interfere with a future, lasting goal.
May I always keep before me your promises
  of the rewards for perseverance:
  abundant fruit, untold blessings,
  and immortality.

God, Eternally Patient One,
    continue to call me,
    seek me, bother me.
For you are the God of Perseverance,
    and that is my hope for salvation.
Amen.

F**reedo**M

Letting the Goodness Out

No man is free who is not master of himself.   —Epictetus

✳ *Freedom is the power to give self permanently in love.*
                                            —Paul Hinnebusch, OP

The more liberated one feels, the less one needs.   —Henry Miller

---

In the previous chapter we saw that discipline was one of the components of perseverance. We are now ready to look at the next trait of a healthy spirituality, freedom. (I must confess that I have an ulterior motive for talking about freedom. I have always been keenly interested in the topic since my family name, Svoboda, in Czech means freedom!)

A chapter on freedom flows naturally from our discussion of discipline, for the two concepts are closely related. Many people would probably view freedom as the opposite of discipline. Ask school kids, for example, what discipline means and many would probably say something like this: "Discipline is doing what my parents and teachers tell me to do. It's not having the freedom to do what I want to do." But if we look at freedom more closely, we will see that freedom is not discipline's opposite. Freedom is discipline's aim.

Actor Ricardo Montalban expressed this natural affinity between freedom and discipline when he said, "Only through self-discipline can we achieve true freedom." Using the analogy of water and a cup, he said, "Pour water into a cup, and you can drink. Without the cup, the water would splash all over. The cup is discipline."

Both of my brothers happen to be pilots. Once, when I was excited about the prospect of flying somewhere, they teasingly said to me, "Remember, Melannie, every landing is a controlled crash!" In other words, without the pilot's control, every landing would be a crash. The control is discipline.

Two images: water being poured into a cup and a jumbo jet landing smoothly onto a runway. Both show us the interplay between discipline and freedom. Discipline channels our freedom, thus preventing our lives from splashing out all over the place wastefully. Or, if you prefer, discipline guides our energies, thus enabling us to make a safe, smooth and purposeful landing. Since we already talked about discipline in the previous chapter, we will now turn our attention to the ultimate purpose of discipline: freedom.

Being Free to Love

Thomas Merton, in one of his lectures to his novices, spoke about freedom. He said, the important question in life is not, "Am I happy?" Rather, it is, "Am I free?" He goes on to say this: "The big question of freedom is: how do I let the goodness out?" In other words, how do I let the love that is inside of me out? Michel Quoist, another spiritual writer, agrees with Merton when he writes, "Freedom doesn't mean being free for nothing. It means being free to love."

What things can inhibit our freedom? What can prevent us from letting the goodness out? Many things can. Take for example addictions. Individuals addicted to crack, heroin, or any other drug, are not free. So overpowered are they by their need for the drugs, they will do virtually anything to get their next fix—lie, cheat, steal, even kill. Similarly, the alcoholic is no longer free either. He or she makes promises to cut down on the drinking, for example, but fails to keep them, because the alcohol proves stronger than the person's good intentions.

There are other things besides addictions that can inhibit our freedom to love. Bad habits can. Perhaps we have the habit of being lazy. Or maybe we have a terrible temper and have made no effort to control it. Or we have the habit of thinking only of ourselves, of being sarcastic, of telling lies. We may excuse our bad habits by saying, "That's just the way I am." But by doing so, we surrender our freedom to change for the better. We allow our bad habits to dictate our behavior. This is easy enough to do, for as the Spanish proverb says, "Habits are first cobwebs, then cables."

There are other factors that affect freedom. Ignorance can. There's an old humorous cowboy song entitled, "I Didn't Know the Gun Was Loaded." The singer of the song begs her friend to forgive her for shooting him, claiming it was an accident and, therefore, not a free act. Fear can also inhibit freedom. If someone puts a gun to my head and orders me to do something, I am not acting freely.

The question is, then, how do we grow in freedom? How do we grow in our ability to love? The answer is simple: we grow by realizing and really believing we are loved by God. We learn to love by being loved. There is no other way.

The Ten Commandments

Someone has said we have thirty-five million laws to enforce the Ten Commandments. I would like to turn to those Ten Commandments now and look at them in terms of freedom and love. In doing this, I am indebted to my former teacher and current friend, Demetrius Dumm, OSB, for some of his insights into this matter.

In his book *Flowers in the Desert*, Dumm reminds us that the primary biblical image of sin is not dirtiness; it is bondage or slavery. Simply put, sin means not being free. Hence, the primary biblical image of salvation is not cleanliness—the "Immaculate Conception" notwithstanding. It is liberation. The story that best illustrates the essence of salvation is the story of the Exodus. We are probably all familiar with the basic facts. The Israelites were slaves in Egypt. In their misery, they cried out for help. God heard their pleas and decided to have pity on them. He enlisted Moses to lead the Israelites out of Egypt and into the Promised Land, that is, out of their bondage and into freedom.

To a very real extent, the story of the Exodus is our story too; for we, like the Israelites, are all held in some form of bondage, no matter how free we may be or think we are. Our bondage can be physical, psychological, or spiritual. Perhaps our bondage is one of the addictions or bad habits mentioned earlier. Or maybe it consists of feeling unappreciated, of being unable to forgive, of being plagued by guilt or anxiety. Even good-hearted people can suffer from bondage if they are slaves to the expectations of others or to the need to be needed. Whatever form our bondage takes, acknowledging it and asking God's help is the first step toward liberation.

In the story of the Exodus, God leads the Israelites out of Egypt. While they are in the desert, God makes a covenant with them, a pact. The Ten Commandments are part of God's "deal" with the Israelites and, by extension, with us. What exactly are the Ten Commandments? Father Dumm calls them the ten "guidelines for freedom." They are God's directives for how the Israelites are to use the freedom God has given them. The Ten Commandments are God's way of saying to the Israelites, "I have loved you into freedom; here's how you are to love others into freedom too!"

According to Dumm, the Israelites' freedom "derives from the experienced love and goodness of God." In other words, their freedom, like ours, is a direct result of their experience that God is good and that God loves them. Only individuals who have experienced God's love and goodness (no matter in what form or even how faintly) are ready to live the demands of the Ten Commandments. For only those individuals who know and trust God enough can risk reaching out to others in love.

Jesus and Freedom

There was no one more free than Jesus. Throughout the gospels, we see him demonstrating over and over again his freedom to love others, his freedom to let the goodness out. Jesus was so free, he could risk loving all kinds of people: man and woman, Jew and Gentile, young and old, rich and poor, healthy and sick, educated and uneducated, spunky and timid, beautiful and ugly, saint and sinner, friend and enemy. We might ask ourselves, "How free am I to love the vast array of individuals God puts into my life?"

Jesus loved people into freedom. In other words, his love liberated individuals, enabling them to be free to love others. When he released individuals from the physical bondage of sickness, for example, Jesus simultaneously released them from their slavery to sin. On more than one occasion he told the newly healed individual to, "Go and sin no more." In other words, be free from the bondage of sin. At other times Jesus gave the healed person a specific mandate to share his or her experience of God's goodness with others. The point in doing this is clear: we can be strengthened in our own belief in God by listening to the faith experiences of others—and vice versa.

But, paradoxically, Jesus was never more free than when he hung on the cross on Calvary. Calvary was the ultimate test of his belief in the goodness and love of God, because it was the place where God's goodness and love seemed the most absent. But so strong was Jesus' conviction in God's undying love for him, he was free enough to surrender everything—even life itself.

In his letter to the Galatians, Paul encouraged us with these words, "Christ set us free; so stand firm and do not submit again to the yoke of slavery" (Gal 5:1). Our struggle for freedom will be an ongoing one. As we journey to the Promised Land, we will suffer periodic setbacks—those times when God's goodness and love seem totally absent in our lives, or times when, due to our anger, fear, or pain, we refuse to let the goodness out. But even these times should not discourage us for, as Gerard Broccolo reminds us, holiness does not consist solely in achieving liberation, "it is also the paschal process, the dynamic movement, the struggle for that liberation."

Questions for Reflection

1. What do you think of the three quotations at the beginning of this chapter?

2. How would you define true freedom?

3. Can you resonate with any of the factors mentioned here that inhibit freedom? Can you think of any others?

4. Think of someone who reflects for you the goodness and love of God. How does this person do that?

Practice
I will use God's gift of freedom today to love someone in a specific and concrete way.

I Ask for Freedom

Loving God,
    I ask for the gift of freedom
    to let the goodness out.
Help me to identify those things in my life
    that inhibit my freedom,
    whether they be glaring addictions
    or more subtle compulsions.
Let me not use,
    "That's just the way I am,"
    as an excuse for not trying to change.
Let me see that the Exodus story
    is my story too;
    and that my liberation begins with
    acknowledging my bondage
    and asking for your help.
Lead me to see the Ten Commandments
    as guidelines for loving.
Make me more and more like Jesus,
    free to surrender everything
    to you—even life itself.
And finally, dear God,
    remind me that holiness
    consists not solely
    in achieving freedom,
    but also in the very struggle for liberation.
Amen.

L OV E

Six Sure and Simple Statements

Love is not an emotion. It is a policy. —Hugh Bishop

I am helpless before love. I could be bribed by a sardine.
—St. Teresa of Avila

To love someone is to reveal to them their value and help them discover that they are precious. —Jean Vanier

---

Love is the perennial "hot topic." It is the subject of poetry, novels, theological treatises, self-help books, songs, sermons, commercials, college courses, and TV talk shows. Love is also the subject of countless proverbs (some of them amusing) from cultures all over the world. Here is a sampling:

- "Two things a man cannot hide: that he is drunk and that he is in love." (Greek)
- "The heart carries the feet." (Hebrew)
- "We are all mortal until the first kiss and the second glass of wine." (Italian)
- "It is as foolish to let a fool kiss you as it is to let a kiss fool you." (Irish)
- "Love quickens all senses except the common." (English)

In looking at love as a trait of a healthy spirituality, I will change my format a little. This chapter will consist of six statements about love with a brief explanation of each one. These statements in no way exhaust the topic of love, but are meant solely to be a catalyst for your own prayer and reflection.

1) God loves us. These three little words summarize the entire Bible. In fact, scripture is nothing less than a love story—a God's-love-for-us story. It is one long and rather convoluted tale of how much God cares for us, thinks about us, respects us, worries about us, cherishes us, gets a kick out of us. God's love is expressed in beautiful words such as these from the prophet Isaiah: "Can a woman forget her nursing child, or show no compassion for the child of her womb? Even these may forget, yet I will not forget you" (Is 49:15). God's love is also expressed in powerful deeds—most notably creation, the Exodus, and the life, death, and resurrection of Jesus.

God loves us. This means that God is on our side, in our corner, and even the president of our fan club. And, as St. Paul asks, "If God is for us, who is against us?" (Rom 8:31) Good question.

2) God loves me. It is one thing to believe that God loves us, that is, humankind, and quite another thing to believe that God loves me. Similarly, it is often easier to believe that God is actively involved in salvation history, than it is to believe that God is actively involved in my history, in my personal and seemingly insignificant little life. But this again is precisely what our faith teaches us. The psalmist sings of God's intimate love for each of us in these words: "For it was you who formed my inward parts; you knit me together in my mother's womb" (Ps 139:13). Jesus, too, stressed God's personal love for each of us—especially when he taught his disciples to pray "Our Father" and when he himself addressed God as "Abba."

3) God loves us (me) no matter what. God's love (unlike ours at times) is unconditional. God does not love us because we are good or beautiful or nice. God does not love us because we tell the truth, floss our teeth, or drop our church envelope in the basket every Sunday. These actions may be commendable, but God does not need them in order to love us. God loves us no matter what. This means God loves us despite the stupid, bad, crazy, selfish, mean, or awful things we may do. How do we know this for sure? Because Jesus tells us so—especially in his parable of the prodigal son (cf. Lk 15:11–32).

The younger son in this parable was a thankless wretch. Not content to get his inheritance when his father died, he pushed to get it while his father was still living. His action reflected his thinking: "I wish my father was dead!" Then, adding insult to injury, the son took his father's hard-earned cash and squandered it away on loose living. When the money ran out and he was reduced to abject poverty, the son came crawling back to his father begging for a job. And what did the father do? He ran out to meet the kid! He hugged and kissed him! He reinstated him into the family! He threw a big party to celebrate his return! Talk about unconditional love! No wonder the elder son was aghast. No wonder he was so put out. We would be too if we thought we were killing ourselves to earn something when all the while it was ours for the taking.

4) Everybody needs love. One of my favorite short stories to teach is "A Rose for Emily" by William Faulkner. It is the story of a proper Southern lady, Emily, a woman so desperate for love she ends up doing something pretty gruesome to get it. I won't spoil the story for you by telling you what sweet little Emily does. The story is not graphic, mind you. In fact, Faulkner is so subtle that there were always some of my students who, after reading the story, completely missed what Emily did. But those who caught it were inevitably appalled. They asked me, "This kind of thing never really happens, does it?" My answer to them was, "Yes, it does" and I pulled out several newspaper clippings with similar stories to prove it.

Then they asked me, "How could *you* like this story?" My answer: "Because it reminds me how much we all need love in our lives—and if we don't get love in legitimate and healthy ways, we will resort to other ways to get it. And I think that's a pretty important thing to know about ourselves, don't you?"

Everybody needs love: newborns (and even pre-borns), the elderly, dentists, police officers, teenagers, parish priests, rock stars, psychiatrists, prime ministers, bag ladies, popes, waitresses, sumo wrestlers, little kids, lawyers—even nuns!

5) *The purpose of life is to learn how to love.* In his book *Hidden Spring: The Spiritual Dimension of Therapy*, Thomas Hart lists this as one of his ten guiding principles toward a healthy spirituality. I agree with him. As was mentioned earlier, Jesus said The Great Commandment was this: "Love God with your whole heart and love your neighbor as yourself." We can infer from this that the very purpose of our lives is to *learn* how to love. The words are carefully chosen here: to learn how to love. Loving is not a skill we are born with—no matter how cute we were as a baby. Loving is a skill we must learn in life.

How do we learn to love? We learn first by being loved. Now, none of us has been or is loved perfectly. None of us has the perfect parents, the perfect friends, the perfect spouse, the perfect children, the perfect religious community. Sadly, some individuals waste their whole lives waiting around for perfect love while missing out on all the other love (imperfect as it was) that is being offered them from many sides—if only they would notice. Even when we do encounter those rare situations where there is no love, we can follow the suggestion of St. John of the Cross, "Where there is no love, put love and you will find love."

Which brings us to the second way we learn to love: by loving. Loving, like all other arts, takes time and practice. That means we can expect to make mistakes along the way. But we don't give up on loving just because we "blow it" a few times. I, for one, am fond of the song that says, "Everybody plays the fool. There's no exception to the rule." Every one of us makes mistakes in loving. That is to be expected. But loving is so vital to human life and so wonderful, it is well worth the time, trouble, and mistakes it takes to learn to do it well.

6) *Love is not easy.* According to Thomas Hart, "Every therapeutic issue comes down to love in some way." People seek therapy or counseling primarily because they are having a problem with love—in one way, shape, or form. That statistic should point out to us how hard it is to love well. If loving were easy, Jesus would have had to say "Love one another" only once. Instead, he said it over and over again in many different ways, using a variety of images and stories, precisely because he knew how hard it was

to do. And still his followers didn't always get the message. Neither do we sometimes.

Questions for Reflection

1. Of the three quotations at the beginning of this chapter, which (if any) appeals to you the most and why?

2. Do any of the six statements about love speak to you at this particular time in your life? Why?

3. Who in your life has taught you the most about love?

4. Can you come up with any other statements of your own about love?

Practice

I will thank God for God's unconditional love for me by sharing my love with someone who could use a little love right now.

God, I Believe You Love Us

God, I believe you love us.
Strengthen that belief.
Let me hear anew your words of love,
    especially as they come to me
    through scripture, through prayer,
    and through the words
    of those who love me.
Give me the eyes
    to see your deeds of love
    expressed in the events of world history
    and in all the little happenings
    of my seemingly insignificant life.
And if I turn from you
    and squander your gifts in loose living,
    may I have the sense and confidence
    to return to your open arms,
    knowing full well
    that your love is far greater
    than any sin of mine.

God, I believe you love us.
Help me to grow in that belief
   through the love of your son, Jesus,
   and the power of the Spirit.
Amen.

G eneratity

Let There Be Life!

*Three things one should do in the course of one's life: have a child,
plant a tree, and write a book.*   —Talmud

*The emptiness many people complain dominates their life comes in
part from a failure to let the world in, to perceive it, to engage it
fully.*   —Thomas Moore

*Here is the test to find whether your mission on earth is finished. If
you're alive, it isn't.*   —Richard Bach

Edwin Chapin, a nineteenth-century American clergyman, wrote,
"Neutral people are the devil's allies." In a lighter vein, John
Holcomb said something similar: "You must get involved to have an
impact. No one is impressed with the win-loss record of the referee."
For our purposes here we could say, "You must get involved to have
a healthy spirituality. No one is impressed with a spirituality that
remains neutral or one that merely judges what is right and wrong,
but does nothing to get involved in making the world a better place."

Rabbi Abraham Heschel wrote: "This is the most important
experience in the life of every human being: something is asked of
me." If we have a healthy spirituality, we probably have had this
kind of experience. We have heard something (or Someone) asking
us to move beyond ourselves and our own concerns, to become
more involved in the critical issues of our day, to have an impact
on the wider world in which we live.

In his wonderful book *Markings,* Dag Hammarskjold describes such an experience: "I don't know Who—or What—put the question. I don't know when it was put. I don't even remember answering. But at some moment I did answer Yes to Someone—or Something—and from that hour, I was certain that existence is meaningful and that, therefore, my life in self-surrender, had a goal." Christian spirituality has a name for this call to self-surrender: it is love. It is a love that proceeds from a deep sense of mission (something is asked of me) and culminates in new life (generativity). Let us look at both of these aspects of love.

A Sense of Mission

What is meant by a sense of mission? It certainly is not that type of proselytizing (more common in the past, but still found in the present) that endeavors to impose its beliefs on others. This is the type that says, "Believe what I believe and do what I say or I'll chop your head off (or I'll take your land away or I'll cut your funding…)." Individuals who operate in this mode have a sense of mission all right, but they have no corresponding respect for the freedom and integrity of the individuals they are trying to influence.

The sense of mission we are talking about here is different from that. It arises out of the conviction that: a) I have received some extraordinarily good news: God loves us, b) I am dying to share this news with you, but c) because the heart of that good news is love, I will always love you even as I try to share that good news with you.

Some might object to this talk of sharing our faith with others. "Faith is a private matter. We should keep it to ourselves," they might argue. Perhaps an experience I had in the grocery store the other day will shed some light on why I think it is not only important to share our faith, it is quite natural.

I was standing by the frozen yogurt case when a young woman, a total stranger, came up and asked me, "Is this brand of yogurt good?" It was a brand I had eaten before and liked, so I replied, "I thought it was good." Without hesitation, she picked up a half gallon of that brand, thanked me, and walked away. A little later I was picking out oranges. Another stranger, this time a young man, came beside me and asked, "Do you know which of these oranges don't have seeds?" I said to him, "I bought this kind last week and they didn't have any seeds." He thanked me and began filling his plastic bag with the kind I suggested.

Because of my previous experience, I was able to give these two strangers my opinion and my help. In one sense, this is what we do when we share our faith with others. We begin with our own knowledge and experience of God's love and goodness, the "good news" of the gospels. Because our faith means so much to us and has helped us immeasurably, we are more than willing to share it with others so they also may experience what we have experienced and know what we know. There is nothing more natural than sharing good news, is there?

Of course, my analogy limps a little. The young woman and man in the grocery store approached me. I did not approach them. And what I shared with them was fairly inconsequential. Yet my point is this: it makes sense in life to rely on the experience and help of other people. If we do this in small matters like selecting yogurt and oranges, shouldn't we also do it when it comes to matters of supreme significance—like our faith?

We can share our faith with others in many ways. Some of us will feel called to share our faith in formal ways such as teaching a religion class or being part of the RCIA program. Others of us might join a Bible study group or prayer group. Most often, though, we will share our faith in less overt but no less important ways: in a casual conversation with a friend over a beer or cup of coffee, in a note of encouragement to someone who is down or ill, in an offer to volunteer at an AIDS hospice or shelter for abused women, or in our presence at the funeral of a friend's parent or spouse.

Generativity

The old proverb says, "Like begets like." Similarly we can say, "Life begets life." If our spirituality is healthy and alive, we will beget life. It is as simple as that. This does not necessarily mean we will beget *physical* life, although, for many people, "begetting" certainly includes having children. It does mean, however, we will beget other kinds of life—especially the psychological and spiritual kind.

Psychoanalyst Erik Erikson defined generativity as "the concern for establishing and guiding the next generation." That definition reminds me of a TV program I saw recently on the Oneida Indians of Wisconsin. I was deeply impressed by their traditional way of making decisions. Before making any tribal decision, they first ask themselves this question: "How will this decision affect the seventh generation?" The *seventh* generation! The Oneida Indians' concern for the seventh generation is an example of generativity at its best!

Jesus begot life. Wherever he went he generated life. He listened to people's stories, healed them of their illnesses, forgave them their sins, fed them bread, offered them hope, laughed with them, wept with them, suffered with them, encouraged them to love, entrusted them with responsibility—thus proving to them they were loved by God and by him. How do we beget life? Just as Jesus did. We, too, are called to listen, heal, forgive, feed, offer hope, laugh, weep, suffer, encourage, entrust—thus proving to people they are loved by God and by us.

It is Jesus himself who calls us to generativity. His beautiful parable of the vine and the branches is one such call (cf. Jn 15:1–10). "Abide in my love," Jesus tells us. "I am the vine, you are the branches. Those who abide in me and I in them bear much fruit." To the extent that we are united with Jesus, we will be fruitful. We will generate new life.

Sister Cleophas

One of the finest examples of generativity I ever encountered was Sister Cleophas, a sister in my religious community. Sister Cleophas taught high school and college math for over fifty years—no small accomplishment. But even more striking than how long she taught, was the way she taught: with incredible competence, undaunted enthusiasm, and remarkable kindness. Although I myself never had her as a teacher, I overheard many students praise her—especially those students who found math difficult. Everyone knew, if you had to take a math course and you hated math or were afraid of it, just sign up for Sister Cleophas' class. She could make anyone understand math—and maybe even like it!

When she was no longer able to teach math, Sister Cleophas eagerly embraced another ministry: she helped organize a group of people to collect day-old bread from a bakery and distribute it to the poor in Cleveland. After a time, even this work became too much for her, so she was assigned to our provincial house in Chardon, Ohio.

I was novice director there during Sister's final years. Small and severely bent over with osteoporosis, she now shuffled down the corridor with a cane. Despite her frailty, Sister was as cheerful as ever and took a keen interest in everything around her. One day, as I was racing down the hall, I met Sister Cleophas. She lifted her head up slowly, smiled, and greeted me cheerfully. I returned the greeting and started to pass by, when something stopped me. Turning around, I went back to her and said, "Sister Cleophas, I want you to know something. Your smile means so much to me!"

Without hesitation and without a trace of self-pity, she replied, "My smile is all I have left to give."

Sister Cleophas knew all about a sense of mission. She knew all about generativity. She bore fruit wherever she went, in whatever she was doing—teaching math in a classroom, distributing bread in the inner city, or simply greeting and smiling at her sisters in the hallway.

(There is a postscript to my story of Sister Cleophas. Several years ago I gave a talk in Cleveland to over two hundred Catholic laywomen, all actively involved in the church. I told the story of Sister Cleophas. After my talk six different women, ranging in age from about thirty to sixty, came up to me. All of them had been taught by Sister Cleophas! And all of them remembered her kindness as well as her competence. These six women were a further testimony to Sister's generativity.)

In an address to the CMSM/LCWR joint assembly, Elizabeth A. Johnson, CSJ, talked about the power of Jesus' resurrection in our lives. Her words seem a fitting way to conclude a chapter on mission and generativity. Johnson said, "God will have the last word in our lives as indeed God had the first, and it is the same word: 'Let there be life!'"

Questions for Reflection

1. Do any of the quotations at the beginning of this chapter speak to you today?

2. How important do you think it is to have a sense of mission? To what extent do you have one?

3. Do you know anyone like a Sister Cleophas who generates life wherever they go? If so, who? How?

4. What are some of the ways you generate life?

Practice

I will generate life today wherever I go and in whatever I do.

Let There Be Life!

Loving God,
 at the dawn of creation you said,
 "Let there be life!"
Let me hear you speak these words
 again today to me.
Renew in me the sense
 that something is being asked of me
 and that my life in self-surrender
 has meaning and a goal.
Help me to find creative ways
 to share my experience
 of the good news with others.
Give me a deep concern
 for the next generation
 and the next and the next...
Help me, like Jesus,
 to beget life
 wherever I go,
 in whatever I do.
Let me hear Jesus say to me today,
 "I am the vine, you are the branches.
Remain in my love
 and you will bear much fruit."
Amen.

Balance

The Role of Work and Leisure

God gives the birds their food, but he does not throw it into their nests. —Greek proverb

The rower reaches the shore partly by pulling, partly by letting go. —Egyptian proverb

Any spirituality that leaves out leisure will lack depth and balance because leisure lies at the heart of prayer, community, and friendship. —Wilkie Au

Several years ago I was asked to give a workshop on leisure and spirituality. As part of my research, I looked in the *Reader's Guide to Catholic Periodicals* to see what had already been written on the topic. I found very few articles listed under *leisure*, but I noticed there were many articles under Lent. Similarly, I found few articles under play, but many under planned parenthood. I found only a few under celebration, but many under celibacy, cemeteries, and censorship. And finally, when I looked under fun, I found no articles but plenty under fund-raising, fundamentalism, and funerals!

The experience showed me how little had been written in Catholic periodicals on a topic I considered integral to the Catholic faith, namely, leisure. (This experience happened several years ago. I am happy to report that today's *Reader's Guide* lists more articles under leisure than it did before.) The fact is, I believe that a wholesome attitude toward both work and leisure is integral to our Christian faith—so much so, that I do not hesitate to designate "the balancing of work and leisure" as one more trait of a healthy spirituality. But what exactly is work? What do we mean by leisure? Let us begin to answer these questions by seeing what scripture has to say.

Spirituality of Work

The book of Genesis tells us several important things about work. First, it tells us that God works. The creation story shows God busy creating the sun and the moon, the earth and the stars, and all living creatures. In the first account of creation (found in chapter one), God works by giving commands: "Let there be light!" and there is. "Let there be giraffes!" and there are. In the second account (in chapter two), God works more directly with creation. God forms Adam out of clay, for example, and then blows life into his nostrils. In this version, God is even depicted as something of a horticulturist, planting a magnificent garden and then placing Adam in it.

This concept of a working God was rare in ancient civilizations. Most people of that time envisioned their gods as *not* working, but rather romping about on mountaintops or lazily lying around snacking and snoozing. But the Hebrew God works. And Genesis makes clear *why* God works. Not because God *has* to, but because God *wants* to. Further, God works not for God's sake, but for *humanity's* sake. So, already in the first pages of the Bible, we see that work is identified with God's free self-giving.

Genesis also shows us how God works. God seems to enjoy it! God is not portrayed as someone who hates his job or sees it as drudgery. We do not hear God complaining, for example, at the beginning of the fourth day, "Darn it! Today I've gotta make those stupid birds! How am I ever going to get them to fly?" On the contrary, God delights in working and, at the end of each working day, pronounces the product of his labors "good."

In Genesis, we also see that rest or leisure is an integral part of the work process. God rests not only on the last day, but also between each working day. We also notice that Adam, like God, works too. God places Adam in the garden of Eden "to till it and keep it" (Gn 2:15). Work, then, is not a punishment for sin, but is one of the ways Adam is made in the image and likeness of God. Through his labors, Adam shares in the creative activity of God.

But something happens to work after Adam and Eve sin. To put it simply, Adam sweats and Eve has labor pains. Perhaps Genesis is saying that, because of the disobedience of Adam and Eve, work suffered too. From that moment on, all work—whether it was cultivating a garden or giving birth to a child—would now involve frustration and fatigue (sweat) and pain (the pain of childbirth).

In summary, Genesis presents us with some fundamental notions about work. Work is essentially good. It is a free act of self-giving expressed primarily in cultivation and care, that is, in bringing forth new life. Even though it sometimes entails frustration and pain, work should basically be satisfying. Rest or leisure is good too, and is somehow integral to the work process.

Spirituality of Leisure

Let's now turn to scripture to see what it says about leisure beyond what we saw in Genesis. The foundations of leisure are found chiefly in the books of Exodus and Deuteronomy. For the Israelites, leisure was identified with the tradition of the Sabbath. This tradition is expressed explicitly in the commandment: "Remember the sabbath day, and keep it holy" (Ex 20:8). What is meant by "keep holy"? The remainder of the commandment tells us: "Six days you shall labor and do all your work. But the seventh day is a sabbath to the Lord your God" (Ex 20:9–10). The implication is clear: "keep holy" means "do not work." But why were the people directed not to work this one day of the week?

The reason is found in Deuteronomy's version of this commandment: "Remember that you were a slave in the land of Egypt, and the Lord your God brought you out from there with a mighty hand and an out-stretched arm; therefore the Lord your God commanded you to keep the sabbath day" (Dt 5:15). This commandment refers to the Exodus event. And it is for this reason that the Israelites were directed to refrain from work on the sabbath in order to use that day to remember how God had delivered them from their bondage in Egypt. In his book *Confessions of a Workaholic*, Wayne Oates says that the chief motive for keeping the sabbath "is not fear of God, nor the need to hew the line of ritualistic practice. Rather, it is the motive of gratitude for deliverance from slavery, gratitude for the gift of freedom."

But the Israelites were to do more than set aside one day a week to thank God for their gift of freedom. They were to express their gratitude to God by the way they worked; that is, by the way they used their freedom all week long. Just as God had used his freedom to free the Israelites from slavery in Egypt, they, too, were to use their freedom to free others from slavery—the slavery of ignorance, poverty, hunger, ill health, fear, old age, or whatever other form slavery can take.

The Sabbath tradition included more than the Sabbath itself. The Israelites were also commanded to observe certain feastdays—most notably the Passover—as well as to celebrate years of jubilee. During a jubilee year there was no planting or harvesting of crops. The land was allowed to lie fallow during that year thus giving it a needed rest. In addition, people who were in debt were allowed to use portions of the land to raise crops in order to pay off their debts. The primary purpose of a year of jubilee, then, was freedom. The year was designed to free the poor from the very real slavery of indebtedness and to free the rest of the people from the potential slavery of greed.

Jesus, Work, and Leisure

There is no doubt that Jesus worked. The people of his day referred to him as "the carpenter's son"—in other words, the son of a common laborer. Tradition says that Jesus himself might have been a carpenter by trade too. Since he did not begin his preaching ministry until he was about thirty, chances are he spent those early years doing what everyone else had to do: work for a living. During his public ministry, Jesus worked too. He spent long hours preaching in synagogues, healing the sick, teaching the masses, conversing with individuals, and traveling by foot from village to village. His work was characterized by self-giving and it offered freedom to those held in bondage by ignorance, illness, or sin.

Jesus worked so hard that he sometimes got exhausted—so exhausted that he once fell asleep in a boat and would have continued to sleep right through a violent storm if his terrified friends had not awakened him. On another occasion Jesus said to his weary apostles, "Come away to a deserted place all by yourselves and rest a while." And Mark explains, "For many were coming and going, and they had no leisure even to eat" (Mk 6:31).

But Jesus balanced his work with leisure. He worked his first miracle not while he was preaching, but as he drank and danced at a wedding party. Often throughout the gospels he is shown dining leisurely with various people. Jesus took regular time out from his busy schedule for another leisure activity: prayer. Over and over again Jesus is shown going off by himself to converse with God in prayer. It is as if those times of prayer gave direction to his work and strength to his soul.

What does all of this have to do with us? Perhaps we can answer that question by taking a few moments of leisure to reflect on these questions: What is my attitude toward work? Do I see it as self-giving and as a share in God's creative activity? How does my work free others from slavery? What is my attitude toward leisure? Do I regularly set time aside to remember God's goodness toward me? Am I able to find God both in my work and in my leisure?

Every Sunday, the new Sabbath, we celebrate Jesus' passing over from death to new life. This observance is more than a commemoration of a past event. It is a celebration of what God, through Jesus, is doing for us right now: freeing us from the bondage of sin and death. With Leonard Doohan we can say, "It is not by work that we earn salvation, but in leisure that we appreciate that it is a gift."

Questions for Reflection

1. What do you think of the three quotations at the beginning of this chapter?

2. Genesis shows God enjoying his work. Do you enjoy the work you do? Why or why not?

3. What are some concrete ways you are trying to balance work and leisure in your life?

4. How can you celebrate the Sabbath?

Practice
I will take leisure time today to enjoy my family and/or friends.

Help Me to Balance Work and Leisure

Dear God,
    help me to balance work and leisure
    in my daily life.
Give me a wholesome attitude toward work,
    one that sees work
    as essentially good,
    as a way of sharing in your own creative activity,
    as a way of giving myself in love
    to others.
Give me a wholesome attitude toward leisure too,
    one that sees leisure
    as an integral part of the work process,
    as a time to thank you
    for your great goodness toward me,
    and a time to decide
    how I might best use your gifts
    to benefit others.
Through the balancing of work and leisure
    may I renew my strength
    and sense of purpose in life.
God, I ask for these things,
    through your son Jesus Christ,
    who knew so well
    how to work and how to play.
Amen.

PrayeR

The Meeting of Two Loves

If you are too busy to pray, you are too busy.   —Anonymous

With me, prayer is a lifting up of the heart, a look towards heaven, a cry of gratitude and love uttered equally in sorrow and joy; in a word, something noble, supernatural, which enlarges my soul and unites it to God.   —St. Thérèse of Lisieux

A Bible that is falling apart usually belongs to someone who is not.
    —Anonymous

On his way out to recess one day, nine-year-old Bobby said to his teacher, "Sister Michelle, could you please say a prayer for me today?"

"Sure, Bobby," Sister said. Then she asked, "Do you have a problem or some special reason you want me to pray for you?"

"No," the boy replied. "I just thought it would be neat to have someone who talks to God every day talk about me."

Bobby was only nine, yet he knew something very important about his teacher: she was someone who talked to God every day. She was someone who prayed.

Anthropologists tell us that all religions, from the most ancient and primitive to the most current and sophisticated, are founded on the belief that being in contact with a deity is absolutely essential for life. This means that all religions espouse some sort of prayer. Our Christian religion is no exception. In fact, one of the most definitive traits of a healthy Christian spirituality is prayer.

Some Definitions of Prayer

What is prayer? Some of us are old enough to remember the definition of prayer given in the old *Baltimore Catechism:* "Prayer is the lifting up of our mind and heart to God." That is not a bad definition, for it reminds us that prayer involves two people: God and ourself. Also, prayer includes two aspects of ourself: our mind and our heart, that is, our thoughts and our feelings and not just one or the other. Still, this catechism definition falls short, for it implies that prayer is a one-way street: it's our sharing with God. This definition doesn't say anything about God's sharing with us.

Another simple definition of prayer is this: conversation with God. Since a true conversation is a two-way street, this definition implies that when we pray we talk to God and God talks to us. Still, this definition is inadequate too, for prayer goes beyond mere talking.

One of my favorite definitions of prayer was given by Catherine de Hueck Doherty who wrote: "Prayer is love. It is love expressed in speech, and love expressed in silence. To put it another way, prayer is the meeting of two loves: the love of God and our love." A good friend of mine once described prayer in a similar way. She said, "Prayer is being in the presence of someone I love and who loves me."

Why Pray?

Which brings us to a very important question: why do we pray anyway? If God is all-knowing, as our faith tells us God is, then why bother to pray? After all, God already knows what's on our minds and in our hearts, so why should we waste time telling God what God already knows?

There are two answers to this question. First, *God* may know what's on our minds and in our hearts, but do we know? Life can get so busy and so hectic at times that we easily lose touch with our thoughts and feelings. Prayer is our "time out" from the busyness of life to reflect on our deeper needs and desires. One reason we pray to an all-knowing God, then, is this: to discover what is really on our mind and in our heart. Honest prayer helps us do that. And why is it so important to get in touch with our deepest needs and desires? Because that's precisely where God usually speaks most clearly to us.

Another reason we pray is not only to discover what *we* think and feel, but also to learn what God thinks and feels. As we said earlier, prayer is a two-way street. When we pray, we give our all-knowing God a chance to communicate with us. This is risky business. All prayer is. By inviting God to speak to us, we risk being changed; that is, we risk having our attitudes altered, our perspectives broadened, our plans modified. And, if we are honest with ourselves, most of us resist change. As the popular poster says, "The only person who welcomes change is a wet baby!"

I was counseling a woman once who, as a child, was abused by her parents who are now deceased. For years this woman clung to her hatred for her parents. Eventually she stopped praying. When I asked her why she no longer prayed, she said simply, "I'm afraid if I pray, God will somehow convince me to forgive my parents, and I can't do that—not yet." I admired her honesty. Her words also told me she knew exactly what prayer could lead to: God somehow convincing her to change, in this case, to forgive her parents, something she clearly did not want to do—at least "not yet." (This woman's "not yet" gave me hope that, in time, she might make herself available to God's convincing love. I heard later she did.)

Quotes on Prayer

I collect quotes. In fact, I have hundreds of file cards filled with quotations that I have gathered over the past twenty years or so. Under the heading "prayer" I have a hefty clump of cards. For the last part of this chapter, I would simply like to share five of my favorite quotes on prayer and say a few words about each of them.

1) Pray as you can and do not pray as you can't. Take yourself as you find yourself; start from that (Dom Chapman). This is excellent advice. If today we don't feel like praying, that's okay. We start our prayer with that. Maybe on another day we feel depressed or we're worried about something. That's fine too. We bring those thoughts and feelings to our prayer. Or maybe we're very busy or very happy about something. That's good too. Wherever we find ourselves today, we start our prayer from there.

2) *God walks amid the pots and pans* (St. Teresa of Avila). Sometimes we think we have to go somewhere special to pray— for example to church, to a park, or to a retreat center. Although it is good on occasion to find places that are very conducive to prayer, the fact remains: any place can be a good place for prayer. We can pray in the car on our way to the mall, at the bank while standing in line, at the kitchen sink as we do the dishes, or even in the bathtub. Most of us learned as little children that God is everywhere. This means that prayer can be everywhere too.

3) *Of all things we do, prayer is the least practical* (Abraham Heschel). Sometimes we see the results of our prayer. Maybe we receive a favor we asked for, or we get the grace to do something difficult, or we experience consolation. When this happens, we thank God, of course. But we do not pray in order to get results. The truth is, most of the time we will not see any results of our prayer—but that's perfectly okay. For we do not pray to get results. We do not pray to get anything. We pray to love Someone. We also pray to become someone: the person God is calling us to be. Ordinarily we become that person not by dramatic leaps and bounds, but rather by barely noticeable baby steps.

4) *The only way you can fail at prayer is to not show up* (Thomas Keating). If we keep showing up for prayer, we have not failed at prayer—even if we feel our prayer is inferior, difficult, or boring. If we persevere in prayer, that in itself is a wonderful grace. In this regard we should remember that when we read all the teachings of Jesus on prayer, we find one recommendation repeated constantly: perseverance. The only person who prays well, then, is the one who keeps showing up for prayer, the one who perseveres.

5) *A lot of trouble about prayer would disappear if only we realized—really realized—that we go to pray not because we love prayer, but because we love God* (Hubert van Zeller). In everything I have said about prayer, we must remember that prayer is not an end in itself. It is only a means to an end. The end of prayer

is love of God and the fulfilling of God's will. The end is, as I quoted earlier, "the meeting of two loves."

In conclusion, we can say that our spirituality is healthy if we pray. It is a good sign if, despite our struggles with prayer, we somehow cannot silence the nagging need to communicate with God on a regular basis. Our prayer will probably take many forms. At times it with be private; at other times we will pray in the company of others. On some days our prayer will be consoling. And that is good. On other days it will be disturbing. And that is just as good, for it could be a sign that we are not merely listening to some idol of our own fashioning, but we are in touch with the unbelievably loving and incredibly demanding God of Abraham, Moses, Mary of Nazareth, and Jesus himself.

Questions for Reflection

1. Read the three quotations at the beginning of this chapter. What do you think of them?

2. Of all the other quotations used in this chapter—especially the five at the end—which one do you like best and why?

3. How would you define prayer?

4. What helps you to pray?

Practice

I will converse with God about my prayer today.

Teach Me to Pray

Loving God, teach me to pray.
Teach me to lift my mind and heart to you,
    to converse with you,
    to allow a meeting of our two loves.
Help me to be honest in my prayer,
    expressing to you
    my deepest needs and desires.
Help me to keep showing up for prayer
    even when I think my prayer is inferior,
    difficult, or boring.

Keep reminding me
    that any place is a good place
    to converse with you.
God, I thank you for the times
    my prayer has been consoling,
    and I thank you for the times
    it has been disturbing—
    those times you have invited me
    to change my mind, my attitude, my plans.
And may I always remember
    that I pray not to get results,
    but to love you
    and to become the person
    you are calling me to become,
    step by baby step.
Amen.

Forgiveness

The Final Form of Love

If God were not willing to forgive sin, Heaven would be empty.
—German proverb

He who cannot forgive others, breaks the bridge over which he must pass himself.   —George Herbert

Marriage is three parts love and seven parts forgiveness.
—Langdon Mitchell

Father Titus Brandsma, a Dutch Carmelite, was arrested by the Nazis in 1942 for warning Dutch journalists not to publish Nazi press releases. Six months later at the Dachau concentration camp, he was executed by a lethal injection. To the nurse who gave him the injection, he gave his rosary and told her he forgave her.

In another instance, a twelve-year-old Cleveland boy was shot and killed by a seventeen-year-old gang leader as the boy played outside in his frontyard. The boy's father was also shot in the back and arm, but recovered from his injuries. Seven months later, when the trial began, this man shuffled into the courtroom and said these words to the judge: "Judge, that boy killed my son. My only son. He wounded me too. But, Judge, I don't hate that boy. I don't hate anyone. I try to be a religious man. I don't believe in an eye for an eye, a tooth for a tooth. I have forgiven that boy, and I don't want him to stand trial and then be sent to the electric chair."

Similarly, a woman wrote to Ann Landers to thank her for a column she published eight years before: "It was the 'forgive and forget' answer you gave a woman with small children and a husband with a 'wandering eye.' You said, 'Don't be stubborn or proud. Take him back. I promise you won't regret it.'" The woman said she had been in a similar situation eight years ago and had forgiven her husband and had taken him back. She ended with, "These past eight years have been our happiest."

These are the kind of true stories I use in my religion classes to talk about forgiveness. The stories never fail to elicit from my students a wide range of strong responses like these:

"How could you ever forgive someone who kills you or kills your only son or cheats on you?"

"I think it's wrong to forgive people. They deserve to be punished for what they did!"

"I admire people who can forgive others, but I know I could never do it!"

In all my years of teaching high-school religion, Jesus' teaching on forgiveness was one of the topics that inevitably aroused the most heated debates in my classes. (It was right up there with issues in sexual morality!) Forgiveness is central to our Christian faith; it is also another trait of a healthy spirituality. In this chapter, we will look at forgiveness from these three aspects: 1) as gospel imperative, 2) as challenge, and 3) as gift.

Forgiveness as Gospel Imperative

If the gospels are insistent about anything, it is the necessity for forgiveness. Jesus says to his disciples, "If you forgive others their trespasses, your heavenly Father will also forgive you; but if you do not forgive others, neither will your Father forgive your trespasses" (Mt 6:14–15). On another occasion he told them, "Be merciful, just as your Father is merciful....Forgive, and you will be forgiven" (Lk 6:36–37).

Jesus linked the forgiveness of others with the worship of God. He told his followers that if they went to the temple to pray and remembered a grudge they were holding against someone, they should leave their gift at the altar and go and be reconciled first (cf. Mt 5:23). The implication is: reconciliation is a prerequisite for worshipping God. Or perhaps the implication goes even further: forgiveness itself is a form of worship.

So unheard of was this emphasis on forgiveness in Jesus' day, that his disciples were very disconcerted by his repeated insistence on it. They murmured among themselves, "He can't be serious, can he? There are limits to forgiveness, aren't there?" One day Peter got the courage to ask Jesus about forgiveness in an attempt to establish some sort of reasonable guidelines or logical limits. Peter asked him, "Lord, if another member of the church sins against me, how often should I forgive? As many as seven times?" Peter thought he was being generous! But Jesus answered, "Not seven times, but, I tell you seventy-seven times" (Mt 18:21–22). In other words, there are no limits to how many times we are to forgive. It is easy for us to imagine how shocked the disciples were by these words, for many of us today continue to be shocked by them!

Jesus did more than preach forgiveness, however. He practiced it—most notably on Calvary and after the resurrection. As he hung dying on the cross, Jesus prayed for his persecutors with these words, "Father, forgive them; for they do not know what they are doing" (Lk 23:34). Moreover, after the resurrection, Jesus forgave his disciples who deserted him in his final hours. Unless we, too, try to forgive as Jesus did, we cannot be his disciples.

Forgiveness as Challenge

But forgiving others is not easy. For one thing, forgiveness goes against our natural instincts. Theologian Doris Donnelly expressed this well when she said, "Forgiveness isn't an instinctive response when we're hurt. When we're hurt the instinctive response is to fight back, to retaliate." To confirm this, all we have to do is watch two small children, siblings, playing together. Suddenly they begin to argue about something. Danny gets upset and hits Holly. What will Holly do? She will probably retaliate either by hitting her brother back or by yelling, "Mommy! Danny hit me!" Gandhi knew how difficult forgiveness is when he said, "Forgiveness is the virtue of the brave." Poet Alexander Pope went even further when he wrote these famous words: "To err is human, to forgive, divine." Because forgiveness is so difficult, it often takes time and help.

A woman learned that her twenty-four-year-old daughter had been murdered. For several years she was consumed with hatred for the murderer. At the same time, she felt tremendously guilty for her hatred. Over the years she prayed to God about her lack of forgiveness and even made several retreats. At one point her minister asked if she could at least pray that God would forgive the murderer. Three years after her daughter's death, she was finally able to do that. But it wasn't until ten years later that the woman was finally able to forgive her daughter's murderer. Forgiveness became possible for this woman because she prayed to God and she sought the help of other people—over time.

Forgiveness as Gift

Contemporary psychology places a strong emphasis on concepts such as personal fulfillment and self-actualization. This emphasis can be misleading if it leads us to trust in our absolute ability to grow continually. Such trust contradicts Christianity's belief that we, though essentially good, are burdened by sinfulness which often impedes our growth toward maturity and holiness. The realization of our sinfulness led writer Wilkie Au to say that the final goal of human existence is not fulfillment; rather, "forgiveness is the end point of human life." Reinhold Niebuhr calls forgiveness "the final form of love." Either way, forgiveness is a precious gift.

Forgiveness is a gift because it frees us. Family counselor Earnie Larsen says, "There is nothing that so deadens the soul, or so retards spiritual growth, freedom, and liberation than carrying around a heavy, stinking bag of resentment." Charles Dickens said something similar: "Without a willingness to forgive those who have hurt us, it is not likely that our lives can go on in any meaningful manner."

Forgiveness, like charity, is a gift that begins at home. The first person we must forgive is ourself. This means we must forgive ourself for not always doing the right or loving thing, for not always measuring up to our standards, for not always meeting our expectations. C.S. Lewis wrote, "If God forgives us we must forgive ourselves. Otherwise it is almost like setting up ourselves as a higher tribunal than God."

Forgiveness is a gift we give to others. We can begin by forgiving others for small things—like everyday hurts, annoyances, and short-comings. Such forgiveness prepares us to forgive others for more important and serious failings. As G.K. Chesterton said, "Forgiving means to pardon the unpardonable, or it is no virtue at all."

And finally, forgiveness is a gift we seek from God and others. Perhaps the two most difficult words to say are "I'm sorry." In fact, columnist Erma Bombeck maintains that "There is only one thing harder in this world than forgiving. It's to ask forgiveness armed only with, 'I'm sorry.'"

When asking forgiveness is difficult, we can remember this humorous incident from the life of Martin Luther. One day Luther lost his temper with an overly virtuous monk. He yelled at him, "For heaven's sake, why don't you go out and sin a little? God deserves to have something to forgive you for!"

I am not saying we should all go out and sin a little! But I am saying this: when we do sin, we know that our forgiving God will be there with open arms to welcome us back. May we have the grace to do the same thing for others!

Questions for Reflection

1. Do any of the three quotations at the beginning of this chapter speak to you today?

2. Reflect on the three individuals who forgave others: the priest, the father, and the wife. What do you think of each of them? Which person do you admire the most (if any)? Why?

3. Have you ever had the experience of forgiving someone who has hurt or wronged you? If so, what helped you to forgive? If not, what prevents you from forgiving?

4. Do you agree that "I'm sorry" is sometimes hard to say? Why or why not?

Practice

I will tell someone "I'm sorry" today or extend forgiveness to someone who has hurt me.

I Ask for the Gift of Forgiveness

Forgiving God,
    I ask for the gift of forgiveness.
Let me see forgiveness
    as a gospel imperative
    and as a requisite
    for discipleship with Jesus.
Give me a greater understanding
    of Jesus' words on forgiveness
    and a greater appreciation
    of his example.
When hurt,
    may I not fight back and retaliate,
    but may I reach out and pardon.
When forgiveness seems impossible,
    may I seek your help
    and the help of other people,
    always remembering that forgiveness may take time.
God, help me to see that forgiveness frees—
    not only the person I am forgiving,
    but also myself.
And finally, when I'm the one
    who has hurt someone else,
    give me the courage to say
    those two little words:
    "I'm sorry."
Amen.

Gratitude

Taking Nothing for Granted

Here dies another day during which I have had eyes, ears, hands and the great world around me, and tomorrow begins another. Why am I allowed two? —G. K. Chesterton

Thou hast given so much to me....Give one thing more—a grateful heart. —George Herbert

Mysticism is felt gratitude for everything. —Anthony De Mello

---

Quick! Before reading any further, stop and think of three things in your life that you are grateful for... Did you come up with three? If so, was it easy to think of three things or was it difficult?

If we can readily and effortlessly name things in our life for which we are grateful, we probably have a healthy spirituality. If, on the other hand, we have a hard time finding anything to be grateful for, our spirituality may be in trouble. In order to understand the relationship between gratitude and a healthy spirituality, let's begin by looking at the nature of gratitude itself.

Astronomer Carl Sagan once said, "If you want to make an apple pie from scratch, you first have to invent the universe." He was implying, I think, that we must never take the gifts we have received for granted. We human beings may be proud of ourselves (and rightly so) for coming up with the recipe for apple pie. We can also take legitimate pride in the skills we have developed that allow us to actually make one. But we must never forget this:

---

without apples there would be no apple pie. In other words, we must never take the gift of apples for granted. In fact, we must never take *anything* for granted—from potable water to breathable air, from joints that bend to bones that don't, from political freedoms to caring friends. In fact, a good definition of a grateful person is simply this: someone who takes nothing for granted.

If we have a grateful heart, we will see all of creation as a gift from God. We will see our own personal life in a similar way and will find ourselves frequently thinking, "How lucky I am!" If we are grateful, the words "thank you" will often be on our lips—during our prayer with God and in our conversations with others. In fact, we can go so far as to say that gratitude is the pulse of our Christian faith. If this is so, then why sometimes is this vital sign so faint in our lives?

The Story of the Ten Lepers

To probe this question, let's look at the gospel story that focuses very specifically on gratitude, the account of the curing of the ten lepers found in Luke 17:11–19. Luke begins the story by telling us that Jesus is somewhere between Samaria and Galilee on his way to Jerusalem. As he enters a certain village, ten lepers come out to meet him. Forced by law to keep their distance from people, the lepers nevertheless shout at Jesus to get his attention. "Jesus, Master!" they cry. "Have pity on us!" Jesus does not carry on a long conversation with the lepers, nor does he cure them on the spot. Instead, he gives them a simple directive: "Go and show yourselves to the priests."

The lepers obediently do what Jesus tells them. While they are on their way to the temple, however, they are miraculously cleansed of their leprosy. We know what happens next. One of the ten lepers immediately returns to Jesus to give thanks. Only one. Jesus asks him, "The other nine, where are they?"

We will never know for sure the answer to that question. But if we read Luke's account carefully, we can come up with a few possible explanations. Luke tells us that "one of them, *realizing* he had been healed" returns to Jesus to give thanks. That phrase is worth pondering. All ten lepers had to realize they no longer had leprosy, right? After all, the external disfigurements caused by leprosy were ordinarily quite obvious. So all ten lepers must have at least realized they were no longer lepers. Perhaps Luke is saying that only one realized he had been healed by Jesus. That is, only he saw the connection between his cure and Jesus. Only he traced the cause for his restored health back far enough to the person of Jesus. Thus he returned to give Jesus thanks.

Grateful people are people who see connections. They see the connection between a gift and the giver of the gift. They trace all their blessings back far enough to their ultimate source and give thanks. Gratitude, then, presupposes two things: 1) that we are aware of the gifts we have received, and 2) that we see the connection between the gifts and the giver of the gifts. If we need to grow in our ability to be grateful, maybe we must first take time to get in touch with our gifts. This may mean we take the time to name them. Perhaps we can do this at the close of each day, thanking God for at least a few of the gifts we received during that day.

Secondly, gratitude presupposes that we see the connection between our gifts and other people. I, for example, have the gift for writing, but I also know I had some excellent teachers along the way who both taught me how to write and encouraged me to do so. When I see the connection between my gift for writing and specific teachers like Mrs. Farrar and Sister Mary Luke, it is easy for me to give thanks. Finally, if we are grateful, we see the connection between our gifts and God, the giver of all gifts.

Saying Thanks and Doing Thanks

It is not enough to merely *say* thanks though; we must also *do* thanks. Brother David Steindl-Rast often makes this point in his various writings on gratitude. The story of the ten lepers illustrates what he means.

Luke gives us a vivid description of the one leper returning to Jesus. He tells us the man glorifies God in a loud voice, falls down at the feet of Jesus, and gives him thanks. What a show of gratitude! But notice Jesus' response to the man. He doesn't encourage the man to stay prostrate at his feet. In fact, Jesus doesn't encourage the man to stay at all. Rather, he says to him, "Stand up and go." Those words are very significant, for they show that while Jesus appreciates the man's expression of gratitude, he urges him to go and carry on with his life. In other words, he encourages the man to do something with his gift of restored health. The lesson is clear: it is not enough for us to say thanks to God for the gifts we have been given. We must do something with the gifts God gives us. *Doing* thanks is ultimately the best way of saying thanks.

Gratitude Embraces All of Life

It is one thing to be grateful for the obvious blessings in life: sunny days, good health, an experience of acceptance, the feeling of success, a lasting relationship. It is quite another thing to thank God for the hardships of life: cloudy days, poor health, an experience of rejection, the sense of failure, a fractured relationship. Yet even the hardships of life can be viewed as blessings, for they often strengthen us, help us to reorder our priorities, enable us to grow in compassion, and keep us aware of our absolute need for God.

The grateful Christian is grateful for *all* of life. As Henri Nouwen reminds us, this kind of gratitude is not always easy. "It is a difficult discipline to constantly reclaim my whole past as the concrete way in which God has led me to this moment and is sending me into the future." Gratitude challenges us, then, to face our past—with both its joyful and painful moments—and to discover God at work in the whole of it.

A Grateful Heart

Recently my eighty-year-old father had heart valve surgery. Although the doctors assured us he was in good physical condition for the surgery, they nonetheless warned us of the risks involved. The night before the surgery, I drove from Detroit to Cleveland to be with my father and family. When I arrived at the hospital, I learned that my mother and brother had just left. This meant I had my father all to myself for an hour or so—a privilege I hadn't counted on.

When it came time for me to leave, both my father and I got a little emotional. As I bent over to kiss him, he said to me through his tears, "I'm so lucky! I'm so lucky!" My father's words impressed me. Here he was—on the eve of what could have been his last day of life—and he was saying how lucky he was! As I drove away from the hospital that night, I was very certain of one thing: my father was in good hands. The gratitude in his heart was an irrefutable sign he was close to God.

Questions for Reflection

1. Read the three quotations at the beginning of this chapter. Do any of them speak to you?

2. What helps you to see the connection between the gifts in your life and the givers of those gifts?

3. What are some of the ways you can do thanks with the gifts God has given you?

4. How lucky are you?

Practice

I will do thanks with one of my gifts today.

Thank You, God

Thank you, God, for everything.
Let me take nothing for granted.
May I, like that lone leper in the gospel,
    have the sense to realize
    that I've been healed—and by you.
Help me to see connections everywhere
    between gift and giver.
May I trace all my blessings
    back to their ultimate source: you.
Help me to realize
    it is not enough for me to fall at your feet
    and say my thanks to you.
I must do my thanks too.
I must use my gifts
    in the loving service of others.
And finally, God, help me to be grateful
    for my entire life,

for light and shadow, joy and sorrow,
gain and loss,
knowing full well that you are at work
in the whole of my life.
I thank you, God.
How lucky I am to know: I'm very lucky!
Amen.

playfulness

letting God Be God

In our play we reveal what kind of people we are.   —Ovid

Attachment is the great fabricator of illusions; reality can be attained only by someone who is detached.   —Simone Weil

You do not have to be holy...to see God in all things. You have only to play as a child with an unselfish heart.   —Matthew Kelty

---

A Sunday school teacher asked her children, "Where does God live?" One small boy replied, "God lives in our bathroom. My dad bangs on the bathroom door every morning and says, 'My God, are you still in there?'"

We may smile at this anecdote. On one level it is a cute story that conveys the simple truth of a child's misperception. But on another level, the story conveys a profound truth about the mystery of God. Where does God live? We Christians know our answer: "God lives everywhere." This means then, as strange as it may sound, that God lives even in our bathroom!

If we have a healthy spirituality, we will have a keen awareness of God's presence in the world. This awareness will color not only what we do, but also how we do it. It will give us a sense of freedom that others may find admirable or foolhardy. We Christians have a traditional name for this type of freedom: we call it detachment. For reasons I will explain later, I like to call it playfulness.

Detachment

Detachment in the spiritual sense means "holy indifference." In concrete terms, this means that, even though I may be very involved in all kinds of relationships and activities, I am not controlled by them, I am not enslaved by them. Robert Wicks defines detachment in more contemporary terms when he says it is "the need to uncover our compulsions and attachments in life." Detachment prompts us to ask, "What are those compulsive and addictive behaviors of mine, those attachments, that prevent me from becoming the person God is calling me to be?"

We often think of detachment in terms of sin. We think of detaching ourselves from bad things like pride, jealousy, anger, and lust. But the truth is we can just as easily be attached to good things—for example, a good person or a good cause. Sad to say, some church ministers today are attached to their ministry; that is, they are "addicted" to their work. It should come as no surprise that good-hearted people do fall prey to workaholism, because workaholism can look a lot like dedication!

We strive for detachment not for detachment's sake, but, as Wicks says, "so we can let go of our idols and risk meeting God anew each day." Detachment helps us to let go of anyone or anything that takes the place of God in our lives. Detachment does not mean, however, that we no longer care about people or the world. On the contrary, as Thomas Merton reminds us, detachment helps us "to discover and develop our inalienable spiritual liberty and use it to build, on earth, the kingdom of God."

Playfulness

Earlier I said I prefer the word playfulness to detachment. This is so because, for me, detachment often conjures up images of emaciated, long-faced, black-robed monks meditating in desert caves. Playfulness, on the other hand, conjures up images of laughing children building sand castles on a beach and skipping along the shore. That image of children playing on the beach, reminds me of another story that illustrates why, as believers, we can afford to play.

Once there was a large passenger ship caught in a storm on the ocean. While the ship tossed back and forth and up and down, a small boy was out playing on the deck. A concerned couple went out to him and asked, "Little boy, aren't you afraid to play out here during this storm?" "No," he replied, "because my father is the captain of this ship." As Christians, we can afford to play even during stormy times, for we know that God is the captain of our ship.

The concept of playfulness has scriptural foundations. In Psalm 46:10, for example, we read, "Be still, and know that I am God!" Another translation says, "Pause a while and know that I am God." Someone has suggested that both "be still" and "pause a while" really mean "have leisure." Without too much of a strain, we could say that the line really means: "Play and know that I am God!" These words echo the advice of Larry Eisenberg: "For peace of mind, resign as general manager of the universe!" Or, as Jon Sobrino, SJ, has said, "It is of the essence of faith to let God be God."

Sometimes it is easy to let God be God, easy to play and let go. When things are going well in life, play often rises naturally and spontaneously. Similarly, there are times when it is easy to let go of certain situations, relationships, places, and plans. But other times, play is difficult and letting go proves nearly impossible. And we find ourselves asking: How can I play when there is so much work to be done? How can I play when so many people are suffering? How can I let go when this person (or place or thing) means so much to me? How can I let go when I have invested so much of myself in this relationship (or work or project)?

It may help us if we think of "letting go" as "entrusting to." For detachment means not so much that we *drop* this person, plan, or situation as much as it means we *entrust* them to God. This is what Jesus did—most notably as he faced his own passion. In his book *The Challenge of Jesus*, John Shea tells us that Jesus displayed an amazing blend of joy, courage, and freedom as he met death. Shea describes Jesus' spirit in these words: "It is the celebration of the supper before betrayal and crucifixion, the insistence of the Kingdom of another world while in chains before the king of this world, the talk of paradise while nailed to the tree of rejection." What enabled Jesus to let go of everything—even life itself? According to Shea it was "his joyous trust in the activity of God."

As the popular maxim puts it, Jesus "let go and let God."

In one of her letters, Janet Stuart describes this type of letting go. She says to her friend, "If you let go of all else, and drop, you will find God's love and strength circling you round, and sooner or later a great calm, in what Catherine of Siena so beautifully calls 'the sea Pacific' of Divinity." She adds that this letting go is often accompanied by the experience of "God loving you, bearing you up, and taking responsibility Himself of all that happens to you."

All about Otters

I am a firm believer that the world of nature has much to teach us about the world of the spirit. Take otters, for example. Several years ago I came across a fascinating article on otters by John Yurus in *Country Journal*. The article taught me many things about otters. I learned, for example, that otters are such efficient anglers that they catch their daily three pounds of fish with very little trouble. This leaves them plenty of time and energy for play—something otters do at great length. "The world is the otter's playground," wrote the author, and he went on to describe otters at play. Otters "will spend hours rolling stones, rubbing shells, and fondling sticks for no discernible purpose other than the stimulation they receive from them."

Otters like to touch not only things, but also each other. They are forever nudging, tumbling, and wrestling with each other. If two otters are kept together, they inevitably end up sleeping "in a heap of loops and coils." This playful aspect of the otter's nature, as striking as it may be, is only part of their story though. Otters also spend considerable time roaming the woods, swimming the waters, foraging, fishing, caring for their young, and attending to their territory. The author concludes with this thought: it is easy to see why the otter is "the delight and maybe even the envy of its human observers. The otter knows how to live."

I am not proposing we all become otters! All I am saying is this furry little mammal might have something to teach us about playfulness and about letting go.

In *Lessons of the Heart*, Patricia Livingston describes spirituality as the pattern of receiving and letting go. She concludes with these words: "The pattern of our lives asks of us so much more than we could ever imagine. It also gives us more than we could ever dream. Emptying us until we feel that we have lost all there is to lose. Then filling us a hundredfold, pressed down, shaken together, running over."

Questions for Reflection

1. Do any of the three quotations at the beginning of this chapter resonate with you and your experience?

2. Do you have any compulsive behaviors or attachments that are preventing you from becoming the person God is calling you to be?

3. In what ways might you grow in detachment and playfulness?

4. Can you recall a time in your life when you let go and entrusted a person, place, or thing to God? What effect did this experience have on you?

Practice

I will entrust all my worries and concerns to God today and take time to play.

I Believe You Are Everywhere

God, I believe you are everywhere.
Give me a deeper awareness
     of your active presence in my life.
May this awareness
     enable me to trust you more,
     and to become more free
     of my attachments and compulsions.
Free me from my idols:
     from anyone or anything
     that tries to take your place in my life.
Remind me again
     that the essence of faith
     is letting you be God.

Give me the joy, courage, and freedom
   of Jesus as I face
   my own forms of diminishment.
May I experience you
   loving me, bearing me up,
   and taking responsibility
   for all that happens to me.
Loving God, let me hear you say to me today,
   "Be still...pause a while...
   have leisure...play...
   and know that I am God."
Amen.

Commitment

Standing For and Against

It is our lot in life to be different. Our symbol is the cross, not a Gallup Poll. —Kenneth Untener

The sad truth is that most evil is done by people who never make up their minds to be good or evil. —Hannah Arendt

If you are neutral in situations of injustice, you have chosen the side of the oppressor. If an elephant has his foot on the tail of a mouse and you say that you are neutral, the mouse will not appreciate your neutrality. —Quoted in Social Concerns Bulletin

I came across this limerick a while ago and it seems a fitting introduction to our next topic:

God made a most hopeful beginning,
And man later spoiled it by sinning.
We know that the story
Will end in God's glory;
But at present the other side's winning!

If we have a healthy spirituality, we will have a healthy awareness of sin. This means we will recognize and acknowledge the evil that resides not only in our own hearts (see the chapter on self-esteem), but also in the world around us. This awareness of evil should not overwhelm us or paralyze us. Nor should it cause us to

111

seal ourselves off from the rest of the world in an attempt to preserve ourselves from the taint of its sin. On the contrary, the realization of evil should summon us forth. It should call us to align ourselves on the side of goodness and truth in the ongoing struggle against hatred, violence, greed, dishonesty, injustice, and all the other forms evil can take.

This call to align ourselves with "the good," this call to commitment is one we cannot afford to ignore. When accepting the Nobel Peace prize in 1986, Elie Wiesel, a holocaust survivor, said, "Take sides. Neutrality helps the oppressor, never the victim. Silence encourages the tormentor, never the tormented." Rabbi Abraham Heschel went so far as to say that being neutral was an impossibility. He wrote:

To be

Is

To stand for.

By our very existence we stand for something—hopefully it is goodness and truth.

Religion Begins with a "Have Mercy"

Religion (and we could add *spirituality*), at its best, helps us to take such a stand. Unfortunately religion is not always at its best—a fact that should give us pause. Martin Buber was in touch with religion's potential shortcomings when he said, "I don't like religion much, and I am glad that in the Bible the word is not to be found."

Jesus knew firsthand that religion does not always help us to stand for good. Religion can become an end in itself and thus distract us from attending to the world's ills. His parable of the Pharisee and the tax collector at prayer (Lk 18:9–14) illustrates this point.

The story takes place in the temple area where two men went to pray, a Pharisee and a tax collector. The Pharisee was the epitome of legal observance and official holiness. The tax collector, on the other hand, was a public sinner. The Pharisee took up his position in the temple area (no doubt in a conspicuous spot), and said this prayer to himself: "O God, I thank you that I am not like the rest of humanity—greedy, dishonest, adulterous—or even like this tax collector." Then he began to list the good works he had performed.

He fasted not once a week as the law prescribed, but twice a week. He paid his tithe not merely on the income from his cattle and land as the law demanded, but on his whole income. In short, the Pharisee, though aware of evil in the world, thought it existed in *other* people—from whom he separated himself. (The word *Pharisee* actually means "separated one.") In his efforts to become a good person, the Pharisee had privatized his faith and reduced it to pious practices.

In contrast, we have the tax collector. This man stood off at a distance, doing nothing to attract the attention of other people. He did not even raise his eyes to heaven when he prayed. Instead, he beat his chest and said, "O God, be merciful to me a sinner." The tax collector was aware only of his own faults and failings without comparing himself to anyone else. Simultaneously he recognized his total dependence on the love and mercy of God.

Jesus made the meaning of his parable very clear to his listeners—lest there be any doubt. "I tell you," he said, "the latter went home justified." Religion begins with an awareness of sin, coupled with the belief in the love and mercy of God. But it does not stop there. It calls us to move beyond our pious practices (no matter how praiseworthy they may be) and beyond our private world (no matter how comfortable it is).

Religion as Countercultural

Our spirituality, if it is healthy, will do more than merely console us; it will challenge us. In his book *Beyond Personality*, C.S. Lewis speaks out against the kind of "vague religion" that solely gives comfort while making no demands. Such a religion is "all thrills and no work," he writes, "like watching the waves from the beach. But you don't get to Newfoundland by studying the Atlantic that way, and you don't get to eternal life by just feeling the presence of God in flowers or music."

In the same vein, writer Jack Pantaleo has said, "Jesus is not an aspirin tablet." In other words, Jesus comes not solely to give us relief from our pain. As someone has said, Jesus comes not merely to comfort the disturbed, but to disturb the comfortable. A religion or spirituality that only consoles and does not challenge, runs the risk of being a haven for selfishness.

Just as authentic faith challenges us, so too, will we challenge others to work toward a more just world. In doing this, we will sometimes win friends and supporters. At other times, however, we will win enemies and detractors. Walter Brueggemann, SJ, reminds us that true Christianity is always countercultural. We practice our faith "in an empire that is deeply hostile."

John Staudenmaier, SJ, teaches courses in religion and culture at the University of Detroit Mercy. He, too, acknowledges the hostility that can exist between faith and culture. He writes that "the life of faith in every era takes the form of a holy tension between primordial cultural tendencies and God's endlessly affectionate challenge to learn to live faithfully." If our spirituality is healthy, we will experience this holy tension between our faith and our culture. We will feel at times as if we are swimming against the prevailing current of our day or we are "out of synch" with the rest of the world. Such experiences can be disconcerting, but they may also be indications that we are following in the footsteps of Jesus.

Jesus and Opposition

Jesus experienced opposition to his teachings and beliefs. Members of his own family thought he was crazy and sought to put him away. The people of Nazareth, his hometown, were so angered by his words, they drove him out of town and even tried to push him over a cliff. Jesus also antagonized the religious and political leaders of his time and place. In fact, one of the reasons he was put to death was because he challenged the "status quo" of his day. He advocated nonviolence in a world that worshipped brute force. He proclaimed the equality of all people in a society fractured into classes. He announced the supremacy of love in a culture that deified law. And, as Elizabeth Johnson, CSJ, has said, Jesus died because he offered "a new vision of a redeemed world shaped according to the mutual services of friendship rather than relations of domination-subordination." Jesus spoke out against evil and injustice. And because he did, he was condemned and put to death.

We are called to follow in Jesus' footsteps. This means that we, too, must be ready to speak out against the evils of our own day.

What are those evils? All we have to do is to glance at the daily newspaper or the evening news and we will know them: poverty, violence, dishonesty, racism, pollution, sexism, greed, to name a few. Sometimes, when facing such issues, we may feel powerless. Against the magnitude of such problems, we may find ourselves protesting, "But I am only one person!" That is true, but we must remember: so was everyone else who ever made a difference in this world. Or we might argue, "What can I do with my limited talents and resources?" In this regard I always like to recall what G.K. Chesterton said, "Whatever is worth doing, is worth doing poorly." We do not excuse ourselves from doing something just because it may not be good enough. As the Italian proverb says, "Better can be the enemy of good." In the name of not being able to do something better, we sometimes do not do the good we could do.

I began this chapter with a limerick. I would like to end it with one too:

Some people think faith is so grand
When life goes along as they planned.
They soon change their story
Faith loses all glory
As soon as it makes a demand.

Questions for Reflection
1. Do you agree or disagree with the three quotations at the beginning of this chapter?

2. Is there anything in the parable of the Pharisee and the tax collector (Lk 18:9–14) that speaks to you today? If so, what?

3. Have you ever experienced opposition because of your faith? How did it make you feel? What did you do in this situation?

4. What factors deter you from speaking out or taking action against the evils of our day? What can help you to be more like Jesus in this regard?

Practice
Trusting in Jesus, I will take a stand for goodness and truth today.

To Be Is to Stand For

God, help me to see
that to be
is to
stand for.
Help me to take a stand
against sin and evil,
and *for* goodness and truth.
Let my faith
not separate me from others.
May it move me beyond religious practice
to concrete acts of love.
May my faith not only comfort me,
may it challenge and disturb me.
Give me the grace
to live the holy tension
between my culture
and your call to live more faithfully.
When I feel overwhelmed
by the evil I see and experience
and by the sense of my own powerlessness,
remind me of Jesus
who faced opposition,
suffering, and death
with love and courage
and total trust in you.
Amen.

H<u>o</u>pE

Taking a Chance on God and the Future

With God, go even over the sea; without God, not over the thresh-old.   —Proverb

Nothing that is worth doing can be achieved in our lifetime; there-fore, we must be saved by hope.   —Reinhold Niebuhr

I cannot imagine that I could strive for something if I did not carry hope in me. I am thankful to God for this gift. It is as big a gift as life itself.   —Vaclav Havel

My mother is a lucky woman. In 1937, shortly before marrying my father, she won a new car in a church raffle—a *gray* Ford (not the usual black) with a trunk (not all cars had them back then). After her marriage, my mother continued to take chances—mostly in church raffles. Over the years, in addition to smaller prizes, she has won one thousand dollars on four separate occasions!

My father complains that he, unlike my mother, never wins anything. My mother is quick to say, "John, when was the last time you bought a raffle ticket?" Her question is a good one, for my father seldom buys tickets. My mother, on the other hand, while certainly no compulsive gambler, takes chances regularly.

Taking chances is another trait of a healthy spirituality. By tak-ing chances, though, I do not mean merely buying raffle tickets. Nor do I mean taking ridiculous chances like jumping off a sky-scraper with an opened umbrella or playing Russian roulette with a loaded gun. No, I mean taking chances on the really big and important things in life—like God and the future.

We have a name for taking a chance on God and the future. We call it hope. In this chapter we will explore the virtue of hope by reflecting on these questions: Why hope? What exactly is hope? And what does Jesus tell us about hope?

Why Hope?

There are two main reasons why we hope. The first reason proceeds from logic, the second from faith. The first reason we hope is this: the alternatives are not very attractive. What are the alternatives to hope? Take your pick: despair, fear, anxiety, cynicism, pessimism, and depression, to name a few. None of these alternatives is very appealing—except to sadists. The poet Dante knew how essential hope was to happiness. In *The Inferno*, he puts this inscription above the portals to hell: "Abandon hope all ye who enter here." For Dante, hell is a place of misery primarily because it is a place of hopelessness.

Winston Churchill said, "I am an optimist. There does not seem much use in being anything else." Similarly, we can say, "I am a hopeful person. There does not seem much use in being anything else."

But we who call ourselves Christians, hope for yet another reason: our faith. Christianity is essentially a positive faith. It preaches the good news, not the bad news or even the so-so news. Some of that good news includes teachings such as these: God loves us— really loves us! Jesus died on the cross for us and rose from the dead! Suffering has meaning! Love is stronger than death! God has prepared a place of everlasting happiness for us! With news such as this, how could we be anything but hopeful!

What exactly is hope? The dictionary defines hope as "a desire accompanied by the expectation of fulfillment." Hope, then, begins with our desires. It begins with our *wanting* something. When we hope, we hope for something we do not yet have. We never hope for something we already have—although we can hope to keep what we already have, for example, a wonderful spouse, healthy gums, a steady job, and so forth. But genuine hope always implies a need. And it always looks to the future.

Furthermore, we ordinarily hope for good things. We do not buy a lottery ticket and then say, "I hope I don't win the lottery!"—unless, of course, we see not winning the lottery as a good thing. Similarly, we do not park our car on the street somewhere and then hope it gets stolen—unless we see some good in having it stolen! Normal people hope for good things or at least things they perceive as good.

Hope Is Difficult

Hope is difficult. Why? For one thing, there are so many bad things happening in our world today—depressing and discouraging realities such as violence, poverty, war, hunger, disease, drugs, environmental problems, bigotry, economic instability, and so forth. Knowledge of these realities makes it increasingly more difficult to hope that a better future is possible. But Dorothy Day, who worked untiringly against the discouraging reality of social injustices, once said, "No one has a right to sit down and feel hopeless. There's too much work to do." Hope means more than merely sitting around and wishing for a better future; it means working to make that better future a reality.

Hope is difficult also because we do not always get what we hope for. Sometimes, of course, we get *more* than we hoped for. There is a story about a group of children at a wishing well in a mall. As the children tossed in their coins, they whispered aloud their wishes. "I wish I had a puppy," said one. "I wish I had a doll!" said another. But one little boy tossed in his coin and whispered, "I wish I had a magnet!" Sometimes we spend our days wishing for a puppy or a doll, when God wants to give us something far better: the whole wishing well!

But sometimes we seem to get far less than we hoped for, or even the opposite of what we hoped for. A young couple hopes for a healthy baby, and they get a child with cerebral palsy. A wife hopes for a change in her abusive husband's behavior, and he continues to abuse her. A priest hopes to get assigned to a thriving parish, and he gets assigned to a dying one instead. We do not hope simply to get what we hope for. Authentic hope is far greater than that.

Playwright Vaclav Havel of the Czech Republic said in one of his speeches: "Hope is an orientation of the spirit, an orientation of the heart. It is not the conviction that something will turn out well, but the certainty that something makes sense, regardless of how it turns out." When we seem to get less than we hope for, we may in reality be getting more. The young couple with the ill child may discover resources of love they never knew they had. The abused wife may finally find the courage she needs to walk away from the abusive relationship. The priest may find blessings in a dying parish that he never would have found in a thriving one. We do not always get what we hope for; sometimes we get something better!

Jesus and Hope

Perhaps no other gospel passage addresses hope more directly or more beautifully than the story of the two disciples on the way to Emmaus. The story is found in Luke 24:13–35. It begins simply enough: "Now on that same day" (the day Jesus rose from the dead), "two of them" (two of Jesus' disciples) "were going to a village seven miles from Jerusalem called Emmaus." Let's reflect for a moment on these words. It was Easter Sunday, but the disciples did not know that yet. For them, it was simply the first day of the week—after the worst weekend of their lives! Jesus had been crucified! He was gone! Just like that! Dead and buried! Oh sure, they had heard the women's incredible story about the empty tomb and the vision of angels; but, of course, they had not believed it. They were totally taken up with Jesus' passion and death—understandably so. We can only begin to imagine what the two disciples were feeling as they walked along—their bewilderment, their grief, their unspeakable disappointment. So distraught were they due to what had happened, they could think and speak of nothing else. Luke told us, that while they were walking, they were "talking with each other about all these things that had happened."

Suddenly Jesus appeared out of nowhere and began to walk with them, "but their eyes were kept from recognizing him." Why didn't the disciples recognize Jesus? For one thing, he certainly looked different (to put it mildly!) than the last time they had seen him! For another thing, they were not expecting to see Jesus again. They had no hope that he would actually rise from the dead. Furthermore, they were too wrapped up in their own pain and grief to recognize Jesus. So Jesus asked them, "What are you discussing with each other while you walk along?" (As if he didn't know!) The two disciples stopped in their tracks. They could not believe this man could ask such a question. They said to him (with a certain amount of indignation we can be sure), "Are you the only stranger in Jerusalem who does not know the things that have taken place there in these days?" (When we are in anguish, we have little patience with those who do not recognize our pain.)

Then Jesus asked them, "What things?" That question is one of the most comical lines in the entire gospels. Jesus knew full well what sort of things! After all, he was there—at the very center of them! By asking the disciples that question, Jesus was not playing some kind of a cruel joke on them. Rather, by asking the question, he was giving the disciples the chance to pour out to him not only their disappointments, but also their hopes and dreams, so he could lead them to see that their hopes and dreams had been fulfilled far beyond their wildest expectations.

The two disciples told Jesus the story of Jesus—ironically! They told how he was "a prophet mighty in deed and word," and how "our chief priests and leaders handed him over to be condemned to death and crucified him." Then they said those most poignant words, "But we had hoped..." Yes, the disciples were hoping. They were hoping Jesus was the Messiah. They were hoping he would free them. They were hoping he would heal them. They were hoping he would never die. They were hoping...

Finally, as if he couldn't take their despair any longer, Jesus yelled, "Oh, how foolish you are and how slow of heart to believe all that the prophets have declared!" And he proceeded to go through scripture with them, carefully showing them that it was necessary that the Messiah should suffer. The disciples were amazed at all that he said. When he gave them the impression that he was going on beyond Emmaus, they begged him, "Stay with us!" Jesus did. While at the table that night, Jesus took the bread, blessed it, broke it, and gave it to the two of them. In that instant "their eyes were opened, and they recognized him." As soon as they did, Jesus "vanished from their sight. They said to each other, 'Were not our hearts burning within us while he was talking to us on the road, while he was opening the scriptures to us?'"

They immediately went back to Jerusalem to tell the eleven and the others. Excitedly they recounted their experience "and how he (Jesus) had been made known to them in the breaking of the bread."

The story of the disciples on the way to Emmaus gives us several insights into hope. Perhaps we can summarize those insights in this way:

Hope is the conviction that:
—what seems to be is not always what is;
—where we've been or where we are is not nearly as important as where we're going;
—faith is reborn by walking together,
welcoming strangers, sharing pain and hopes,
searching the scriptures, and breaking bread;
—life, and not death, has the last word;
—and what's really real is more incredibly wonderful than our wildest expectations!

Questions for Reflection
1. What is your opinion of the three quotations at the beginning of this chapter?
2. How would you define hope?
3. What are some other reasons why hope can be difficult?
4. What helps you to be a more hopeful person?

Practice
I will write the words "Hope is the conviction that..." and finish the sentence with God in prayer.

Help Me to Take a Chance

God, help me to take a chance
on you and on the future.
Help me to bet on the good news,

to risk everything,
and to stake my life on Jesus.
Increase my hope
by revealing to me
my deepest desires.
When I am downcast or distraught
by realities inside and around me,
lead me to share my pain and shattered hopes
with others along the way.
Like the disciples on their way to Emmaus,
may I welcome Jesus to walk with me,
and walk me through the scriptures.
Help me always to find new strength
in the breaking of the bread.
God, give me the grace to see
that which seems to be
is not always what is;
and where I have been and where I am
are not nearly as important
as where I'm going:
toward you, I hope!
Amen.

Restlessness

Is This All There Is?

Life's a voyage that's homeward bound.   —Herman Melville

The world is like an inn; the world to come, like home. —Talmud

The best way to prepare for death is to develop a capacity for surprise.   —John Shea

---

There is a cartoon that shows a little boy opening his presents on Christmas morning. He eagerly tears into dozens of boxes, tossing presents and paper everywhere. Finally, after opening the last present, he sits somewhat dejectedly in a sea of wrapping paper and asks his parents, "Is this all there is?"

We are sometimes like that little boy. We, too, have received innumerable gifts in life—family, friends, health, talents, education, opportunities of all kinds—yet periodically we find ourselves asking, "Is this all there is?"

In her book *Teaching a Stone to Talk,* Annie Dillard describes the dissatisfaction we sometimes experience in life. She writes, "I alternate between thinking of the planet as home—dear and familiar stone hearth and garden—and as a hard land of exile in which we are all sojourners." Malcolm Muggeridge believed the "sojourner experience" is essential for Christians. He said, "The only ultimate disaster that can befall us...is to feel ourselves to be at home here on earth." Earthly coziness can kill the spiritual life.

If we have a healthy spirituality, we will sometimes feel that we are, indeed, exiles in a foreign land—no matter how dear earth is to us. We will experience a sense of restlessness or what I like to call a "holy discontent"—no matter how good life has been for us. We will have the distinct impression that there is more to life than anything we already know or have experienced. (And of course, we are right!)

Religious monk Sebastian Moore describes this experience as the desire for "I know not what." He says it is the desire not for this or that particular thing, but for the "unnamable." St. Augustine ventured to name the unnamable when he wrote those famous words: "My soul is restless, O Lord, until it rests in Thee." The ultimate desire of our souls, then, is God. No one else or nothing else can satisfy our longing—no matter how good or beautiful or wonderful they may be. Little wonder we sometimes feel restless and empty. Little wonder we sometimes become impatient with this process called life.

Process as Becoming

There's a popular poster that hangs in many a school that says, "Be patient with me! God isn't finished with me yet!" The poster is certainly an appropriate reminder for teachers who deal all day long with children and youth—those obviously "unfinished products." But the deeper truth is that we are *all* unfinished products. God isn't finished with any of us yet. We are all still in process even if we are over one hundred years old!

Process deserves respect. It also demands patience. We live in a culture, however, that has little tolerance (let alone patience) for process—a culture that can't seem to wait for anything. So hurried are we that we make *instant* oatmeal for breakfast, ride the *Rapid* Transit to work, eat *fast* food for lunch, take our car to *Jiffy* Lube and *Speedy* Muffler, take our work to *Quickie* Printing, and get our hair cut at a salon that promises *no waiting*.

But we cannot rush faith; we cannot hurry matters of the spirit. Martin Luther believed process was integral to the spiritual life. He wrote, "This life, therefore, is not righteousness but growth in righteousness, not health but healing, not being but becoming." If we have a healthy spirituality we will try to be patient with becoming: our own becoming and the becoming of others, for example, our family, friends, coworkers, and neighbors. We will also be patient with the becoming of our local community, our parish, our country, our church. We will keep in mind the words of Dyckman and Carroll in their book *Inviting the Mystic, Supporting the Prophet:* "We do not just 'have faith.' We become trusting, believing, 'faithing' people as we wrestle with the givenness and crises of our lives."

Hunger and Loneliness

Jesus addressed this restlessness, this yearning of the human spirit. In Luke's version of the Beatitudes, he says, "Blessed are you who are hungry now, for you will be filled" (Lk 6:21). Jesus is not talking about mere physical hunger here. That kind of hunger certainly is not a good in itself. Rather, Jesus is referring to that basic fact of the human condition: our innate hungering and yearning for fulfillment. As Demetrius Dumm, OSB, writes, "To be human is to be incomplete, unfinished; it is to be away from home." The pain of our incompleteness becomes a problem only if we try to fill the void with the goods of this world such as material things, power, popularity, sex, work. The pain of incompleteness is a blessing if it keeps us aware of our need for God.

Sometimes the pain of incompleteness takes the form of loneliness. In his book *Reaching Out,* Henri Nouwen distinguishes between the loneliness that can lead us to contemplative solitude and eventually to God, and the loneliness that can drive us away from ourselves and from God. Always the realist, Nouwen writes, "To wait for moments or places where no pain exists, no separation is felt and where all human restlessness has turned to inner peace is waiting for a dream world. No friend or lover, no husband or wife...will be able to rest our deepest craving for unity and wholeness."

Life as a Journey

One way to deal with our restlessness is to think of life as a journey. Chances are the journey metaphor will speak to most of us because we all make journeys in life. Some of those journeys are pleasant ones: driving to our grandparents' home on Thanksgiving Day, going to visit a friend, starting out on a vacation. But other journeys are not so pleasant: going back to school after Christmas vacation, driving to the dentist's office, going to see a friend who is dying. What determines the kind of journey it will be? What factors give each journey its color or texture? Two things: the people we travel with and our destination.

When I was a child, for example, my family always went to my grandparents' home for Thanksgiving. This meant driving from our small farm about twenty miles east of Cleveland to Cleveland's near west side. We drove through the heart of Cleveland (there were no freeways back then), so it was stop-and-go traffic lights the whole way. Often the weather was cold and dreary, and sometimes the heater in the car didn't work right. Yet I remember those trips as fun and exciting—we kids bouncing up and down in the back seat imagining all the goose, dumplings, and kolacky that were waiting for us at the end of the trip. What made this journey so wonderful for me? The companionship of my family and the thought of the destination.

In contrast, the trip to the dentist's office was never wonderful no matter how smooth the traffic, how sunny the weather, how kind the dentist. The image of the dentist's drill cast a pall over everything, proving once again that knowledge of the destination can make or break the journey.

Our life is a journey. Its color and texture are largely determined by those individuals who make the journey with us (family, friends, coworkers, acquaintances) and by knowledge of our destination (our heavenly home). When the journey of life becomes dreary or burdensome, perhaps it means we are not paying enough attention to our traveling companions. Maybe we have mistakenly imagined we can make the journey alone.

Or perhaps our journey has lost its excitement, because we have lost sight of our destination. Maybe we can no longer envision all the love, joy, peace, and excitement that will be ours when we finish our earthly journey and enter heaven.

Heaven: A Room Full of Puppies

We do not read too much about heaven these days, even though the belief in heaven is part and parcel of our Christian faith. Jesus himself speaks of heaven many times in the gospels, often using vivid images when he does. His most consistent and well-known image of heaven is that of a wedding feast, an image that conveys the happiness, excitement, fun, and good fellowship that awaits us there. One way for us to keep our heavenly goal alive is to imagine what entering heaven is going to feel like, based on some of the experiences we have had here on earth. Here's one of mine.

A number of years ago I lived in a boarding school—in a house with another sister and fourteen sixteen-year-old girls. My parents still lived on their farm nearby. One day in March, my father called me and said that someone had dropped off a beagle in front of their house. The abandoned beagle was "very pregnant." Feeling sorry for the dog, my father took her in. Shortly after, she gave birth to six puppies. As cute as they were, my father moaned, "What am I going to do with six puppies?" I came up with a solution: we would find homes for the puppies among our students at school. So, as soon as the puppies were weaned, my father brought them to our house where we put them in the enclosed back porch for the night.

Very early the next morning, I went downstairs, quietly opened the door to the back porch, and tiptoed in. The puppies, who had been sound asleep in a heap, heard me. Suddenly they jumped up, ran towards me, and began jumping up and down and yelping at my feet. They were one frisky body with twenty-four legs and six wagging tales—so full of life, so energetic, so happy to see me! As I stooped down to pet them, they kept jumping, yelping, and licking my face. I remember thinking, "Entering heaven's got to be like this! It's got to be like walking into a room full of puppies!"

Albert Einstein said, "Imagination is more powerful than knowledge." Maybe that is one reason Jesus used so many images when he taught. None of us knows for sure what heaven is going to be like, of course, but we do have these occasional inklings, these timely hints along the way. Heaven is like a wedding feast, a party, Jesus tells us. It is like walking into a room full of puppies, I say.

What do *you* say?

Questions for Reflection
1. What do you think of the three quotations at the beginning of this chapter?
2. Do you ever feel like a "sojourner" on earth? If so, what factors contribute to this feeling? What do you do with this feeling?
3. How patient are you with process? Can impatience sometimes be a good thing?
4. What are some of your inklings and images of heaven?

Practice
I will appraise with God in prayer how I am dealing with feelings of restlessness, discontent, emptiness, and loneliness.

I'm Restless
Gracious God,
    I'm restless.
Despite how dear this planet is at times,
    despite how wonderful life can be,
    I'm still restless.
I hunger, I yearn,
    I crave for more.
Help me to see this restlessness
    as a blessing from you.
Let me not try to ease its pain
    with things of this world.
Help me to be more patient
    with process, with becoming—
    my own becoming and that of others.
May the loneliness I feel at times
    encourage me to reach out to you in prayer
    and to others in deeds of love.
God, give me a deeper realization
    of my life as journey.
May I value my traveling companions.
And may I keep my eyes ever fixed
    on my final destination:
    you, my home.
Amen.

Bibliography

Au, Wilkie, SJ. *By Way of the Heart: Toward a Holistic Christian Spirituality.* New York: Paulist Press, 1989.

Bellah, Robert N. et al. *The Good Society.* New York: Knopf, 1991.
Broccolo, Gerard T. *Vital Spiritualities: Naming the Holy in Your Life.* Notre Dame: Ave Maria Press, 1990.
Brown, H. Jackson. *Live and Learn and Pass It On.* Nashville: Rutledge Hill Press, 1992.

Chesterton, G.K., *Orthodoxy.* New York: Doubleday, 1973.
Conn, Joann Wolski, ed. *Women's Spirituality: Resources for Christian Development.* New York: Paulist Press, 1993.

De Mello, Anthony. *One Minute Wisdom.* New York: Doubleday, 1988.
_____.*Wellsprings: A Book of Spiritual Exercises.* Garden City: Doubleday, 1985.
Dillard, Annie. *Teaching a Stone to Talk.* New York: Harper and Row, 1988.
Doherty, Catherine de Hueck. *Soul of My Soul.* Notre Dame: Ave Maria Press, 1985.
Doohan, Leonard, "The Spiritual Value of Leisure," *Spirituality Today* (June 1979): 164.
Dumm, Demetrius, OSB. *Flowers in the Desert: A Spirituality of the Bible.* New York: Paulist Press, 1987.
Dyckman, Katherine Marie, SNJM, and L. Patrick Carroll, SJ. *Inviting the Mystic, Supporting the Prophet.* New York: Paulist Press, 1981.

Erikson, Erik. *Identity, Youth and Crisis.* New York: Norton, 1968.

Furlong, Monica, "Connect and Collect," *The Tablet* 24 (March 1990): 380.

Greeley, Andrew. *The Friendship Game.* Garden City: Doubleday, 1970.

Hammarskjold, Dag. *Markings.* New York: Knopf, 1965.
Hart, Thomas. *Hidden Spring: The Spiritual Dimension of Therapy.* Mahwah: Paulist Press, 1994.
Heschel, Abraham Joshua. *I Asked for Wonder: A Spiritual Anthology.* New York: Crossroad, 1983.

Kennedy, Eugene. *The Joy of Being Human*. Chicago: Thomas More Press, 1974.
_____. *A Time for Being Human*. Chicago: Thomas More Press, 1977.
Koontz, Dean R. *Strangers*. New York: Putnam, 1986.
Kushner, Harold S. *When Bad Things Happen to Good People*. New York: Schocken Books, 1981.

Larkin, William. *Get Real: 25 Ways to Grow Whole and Holy*. Mystic: Twenty-Third Publications, 1995.
Lewis, C.S. *The Four Loves*. San Diego: Harcourt Brace Jovanovich, 1960.
_____. *Beyond Personality*. New York: Macmillan, 1945.
_____. *Surprised by Joy: The Shape of My Early Life*. New York: Harcourt Brace Jovanovich, 1966.
Livingston, Patricia. *Lessons of the Heart: Celebrating the Rhythms of Life*. Notre Dame: Ave Maria Press, 1992.

Merton, Thomas. *The Sign of Jonas*. Garden City: Image Books, 1953.
Moore, Sebastian. *Let This Mind Be in You: A Quest for Identity through Oedipus to Christ*. New York: Harper and Row, 1985.
Moore, Thomas. *Care of the Soul*. New York: HarperCollins, 1992.

Niebuhr, Reinhold. *The Irony of American History*. New York: Charles Scribner's Sons, 1952.
Nouwen, Henri J.M. *Reaching Out*. Garden City: Doubleday, 1975.

Oates, Wayne. *Confessions of a Workaholic: The Facts about Work and Addiction*. Nashville: Abingdon, 1971.

Pantaleo, Jack, "The Opened Tomb," *The Other Side* 28, 2 (Mar-Apr, 1992): 10.
Peck, M. Scott. *The Road Less Traveled*. New York: Simon and Schuster, 1978.
Pollard, Miriam, OCSO. *The Laughter of God*. Wilmington: Michael Glazier, 1986.
Puls, Joan, OSF. *Every Bush Is Burning*. Mystic: Twenty-Third Publications, 1986.
_____. *Seek Treasures in Small Fields: Everyday Holiness*. Mystic: Twenty-Third Publications, 1993.

Quoist, Michel. *With Open Heart*. New York: Crossroad Publishing, 1983.

Rohr, Richard. *Notes from Simplicity: The Art of Living*. New York: Crossroad, 1991.

Samra, Cal. *The Joyful Jesus: The Healing Power of Humor*. San Francisco: Harper, 1986.
Shea, John. *The Spirit Master*. Chicago: Thomas More Press, 1987.
_____. *The Challenge of Jesus*. Chicago: Thomas More Press, 1975.